RAISING GREAT KIDS

RAISING GREAT KIDS

A COMPREHENSIVE GUIDE TO

Parenting with Grace and Truth

Dr. Henry Cloud & Dr. John Townsend

MOTHERS OF
MOPS
PRESCHOOLERS

ZONDERVAN™

GRAND RAPIDS, MICHIGAN 49530

ZONDERVAN™

Raising Great Kids
Copyright © 1999 by Henry Cloud and John Townsend

Requests for information should be addressed to:
Zondervan, *Grand Rapids, Michigan 49530*

Library of Congress Cataloging-in-Publication Data

Cloud, Henry.
    Raising great kids: parenting with grace and truth / Henry Cloud and John Townsend.
       p. cm.
    Includes bibliographical references and index.
    ISBN 0-310-23549-9 (softcover)
    1. Parenting—Religious aspects—Christianity.   I. Townsend, John Sims, 1952–
II. Title.
BV4529.C54 1999
248.8'45—dc21   98-51434
                                                                    CIP

Published in association with Yates & Greer, LLP, Literary Agent, Orange, CA

Interior design by Sherri L. Hoffman

Printed in the United States of America

---

02 03 04 05 06 07 08 /❖ DC/ 14 13 12 11 10 9 8

To MOPS and all the other parents who give their hearts to raising great kids

Henry Cloud

To Ricky and Benny

John Townsend

Contents

Foreword

At MOPS International—an organization that encourages and supports mothers of young children—we are often asked what resource we recommend on the elusive and challenging subject of parenting.

Well, here it is!

With all the fantastic books and curriculums available today, how can we choose *Raising Great Kids* as our favorite? Three reasons:

First, it works. It speaks the language moms and dads speak. It makes sense. We can *get* this stuff. When I consider the everydayness of parenting, Drs. Henry Cloud and John Townsend provide principles and techniques that work.

Second, it's biblical. With both theological and psychological training to their credit, the authors offer us an integrated and trustworthy perspective. They've done their homework and offer us the results.

Third, it's foundational. This big-picture book covers all the ages and stages of parenting while underlining the unique importance of the early years. As parents, it's great to begin with the end in mind. I can see the results of this parenting approach played out in the character of my own kids. No, they're not perfect. But they are great!

Take this moment from just a few weeks ago as an example.

Our family pushed our chairs back from the iron deck table where we had just consumed my daughter's favorite dinner of grilled chicken, pasta, and veggies. My husband and twelve-year-old son, Ethan, headed out to hit golf balls, leaving the summer evening stretching before fourteen-year-old Eva and me. We lingered on the deck, reviewing her excursions of the past three weeks: summer camp followed by a trip with her church youth group. I missed her.

My daughter, five feet eight inches, is growing up and away. I marvel at the young woman before me. To my surprise, that night she talks—really talks—with me about her life, touching on everything from boys to girlfriends to God. In one moment I recognize a gentle shift between us. Yes, I am still Mom. But I am becoming Friend. She still needs me, but differently than in the past decade. Our relationship nudges forward to a new place. Instinctively I know my daughter has now completed her childhood journey and now sets out in the direction of adulthood. Building on the parenting of her past, she reaches out and around me toward tomorrow. And I watch, amazed.

I remember her bouncy, two-year-old dimpled face, her eager excitement at five, her charming and willing spirit at ten, and her metamorphosis into adolescence just a year later. Now, sitting on the deck, enjoying her teen discoveries, I muse that our bonded relationship, forged in infancy and continuing to change, remains the single most important ingredient in our mother-daughter journey together. Sure, there were "looks" and spankings and time-outs and lectures that helped make her what she is today. But on this summer evening, at this juncture, I sit back in my deck chair, listen to my daughter, and recognize within me the peace of time well spent in a relationship. The nurture of my touch, my eyes focused on her eyes, my ears tuned to her voice, my investment in her from infancy forward are paying off.

So, as the president of MOPS International and as the mother of two growing and going children, I believe this book is the best resource for guiding us through the parenting process from rocking chair to deck chair. Whether you're just beginning your parenting journey, like many mothers of preschoolers, or well down the road, there is help for you here.

ELISA MORGAN
PRESIDENT AND CEO,
MOTHERS OF PRESCHOOLERS (MOPS), INC.

Introduction

A Forbidden Topic

At a retreat at which I (Dr. Cloud) spoke recently, the discussion at the lunch table turned to parenting. At first, people talked about their children. But soon they started talking about particular parenting philosophies and practices. I remembered what my childhood barber once told me: "If you want to stay friends with people, don't talk about religion or politics." I think he should have added parenting to his list of forbidden topics.

As the table discussion progressed, battle lines were drawn. In fact, I was reminded of Buffalo Springfield's classic song of the '60s, "For What It's Worth":

> Battle lines bein' drawn;
> Nobody's right if everybody's wrong.
> People carrying signs:
> Mostly saying, "Hurrah for my side."

Although people were prefacing their remarks with conversational niceties, I could feel the underlying tension.

On one end of the spectrum, my luncheon partners advocated structure and control at the expense of everything else. To raise an obedient child is the most important thing. On the other end, they advocated love over structure. Having a child feel loved and secure in love is primary. Structure plays a secondary role.

Then there were those who emphasized the sinfulness of children. According to them, if you didn't seize every opportunity to focus on getting control of the little sinners, you would lose them for sure. Still others emphasized the inherent goodness and innocence of children, feeling that they only sin when they have been first mistreated by the outside world.

The tone of their voices and the expressions on their faces revealed that each saw the other side as a villain. *Where is this conflict coming from?* I thought to myself. *Why can't they just discuss their viewpoint without vilifying those who disagree?* As I listened further, some things made sense. I understood why there was so much passion around the table.

My luncheon partners were not talking philosophy after all. They were talking about something much closer to home. They were discussing four aspects of their lives in which they had invested their very hearts:

1. Their children's welfare
2. Their community
3. Their own welfare
4. Their God

When I understood the role that each of these "heartbeats" played in their discussion of childrearing, I got it. There should be passion surrounding an issue that touches on the things they care about the most. Let's look at each and see why.

First, in terms of their children's welfare, these people wanted the best for them. What would help their children be healthy now and secure for the future? What discipline would give their children the ability to say no to drugs? What would help them to succeed in school? How do parents make sure that their children grow up to be capable of intimacy and love? What can they do in a child's early years to prevent divorce later on?

For these reasons, parents can hardly stay neutral when talking about parenting practices. After all, what they decide to do might affect several generations, much less the next handful of years. Because parents love their children, parenting philosophy is more than an academic topic.

Second, in terms of community, these parents were not alone. Instilled in their thinking were the admonitions of the people with whom they live day-to-day. Their friends, families, and church groups were all telling them what to do. Many were members of some particular parenting group at their local church, meeting regularly to learn how to be the parents their children need. Others received regular input from their own parents, grandparents, or other extended family. Still others received advice from their close circle of friends and other support systems.

So this topic couldn't be neutral. To entertain an idea about what to do with a crying infant that is different from what the group tells you to do might put you at odds with your closest friends or support system.

Think of the pressure on a young parent who wants to discipline a certain way, or raise a teenager with certain limits different from those of her pastor or her mother. You are no longer just talking about the child. When you parent, you invite conflict with those who care about you and who care about your child.

Third, when one talks about parenting, he is not just talking about his child. He is also talking about his own welfare, or the welfare of his marriage. After all, isn't your life greatly affected by how your children are doing? Don't you want to be able to sleep through the night and not have to feed a crying infant eight times? Don't you want to be able to spend that savings account on a family vacation and not drug treatment? Don't you want to have a loving and playful conversation around the dinner table instead of constant bickering? And don't you want to be able to avoid the broken heart of watching your child live out a life of pain?

So when a parent talks about parenting, he is talking not only about the welfare of the child but about his own welfare also. It becomes understandable why a parent cannot just listen neutrally to a discussion about what to do with an infant or a teenager. The topic concerns him in a very deep and personal way.

And finally—something that would probably surprise my barber—a discussion on parenting styles is a discussion about religion after all. It is a discussion about morals, values, and responsibility to the God who entrusted that child to the parents' safekeeping for eighteen or more years. Try suggesting to a devout believer of a particular philosophy of parenting that this philosophy is just a "secular theory," not really something God would approve of.

Those are fighting words. The discussion can quickly escalate from potty training to whether or not the parent is a "true believer" or a heretic. To change or entertain a new idea threatens a larger belief system and one's own view of true spirituality.

So, with this new understanding, I listened with much greater empathy for the passion with which those parents put forth their arguments. I understood where they came from. I understood that they desperately wanted to raise great kids.

With this same spirit, we have written this book. Not only are we empathetic to parents who struggle with figuring out what is best for their children, but we were also encouraged by Mothers of Preschoolers International, Inc. (MOPS) to offer a guide for parents. All around the country, parents are in discussions like the one I mentioned above. They feel tremendous pressure to do the right thing for their child, for themselves, in light of their community, and before God. It's a daunting task.

With those winds blowing behind us, we set out to take a seat at the table to put forth what we believe about parenting and about the things children need in order to grow into the adults God designed them to be. We, too, are not short on belief. We have tried to build this book around some of the values that are most important to us. Let's look at some of these at the beginning so that you will be able to see them as you go through the book.

The Value of Love

Relationship is central not only to the order of the universe God has created, but also to parenting. You can't construct character in a child without deep relationship with parents. Everything we know from the Bible as well as our own observation tells us that, most of all, children need love. When they come into the world, they are empty and devoid of love, and they must have it to grow. In fact, they can die without it. And if they do not die, they will not thrive emotionally, physically, or spiritually.

In addition, not only is relationship central for their development, but *it is their ultimate goal in life as well.* As Jesus told us, the entire law can be summed up in the law of love. To love

God and to love others is to understand all of the command-ments. A child who grows up obedient and in control, but dis-connected does not grow up at all. She is a shell of a person.

Therefore you will see that, at its core, this book is a rela-tional system. To develop, your child is going to need to be deeply related to you and others, and you are going to have to keep relationship as a goal of her development. We will help you to do that all along the way.

The Value of Truth

But love alone is not enough. We must have the structure of reality and truth to make our relationships and the rest of life work well. Children cannot be loved too much, but they can be disciplined not enough. They need to be able to hear truth and learn how to respond to it, ultimately living their lives in accord with it.

In a child's life, parents are the dispensers of truth and real-ity. Therefore we have tried to show you what kinds of truth chil-dren need at what ages, and how to present it to them. Sometimes we will ask you to tell or teach them; other times we will ask you to discipline them for them to learn; still other times we will instruct you how to let them experience it on their own without your getting in the way. But in all of these ways, the goal is to have your child become a person of truth, living in wisdom.

The Role of Character

Parenting is a temporary job. One day your children will have to go off on their own. After they have gone, the character you built into them will guide them. As Jesus said, a good tree can-not bear bad fruit and vice versa (Matthew 12:33). Therefore you need to be much more concerned about what kind of tree your child is becoming than any particular fruit you might see on a single day.

In light of this, we have always tried to see a particular prob-lem or task in light of the ultimate task of character develop-ment. We want to help you to have not only children who obey, but also children who become people who obey. Anyone can obey with a police officer around, but ultimately, only people of character obey when no one is around to tell them what to do.

So we will instruct you about how to develop character. What do children need from you as infants or as toddlers or as teens to develop character that will take them safely through life? How can you build integrity that will protect them for life (see Proverbs 10:9)? We will help you with that process.

An Understanding of Sin, Immaturity, and the Image of God

There are a few dangerous extremes out there today. Some overemphasize the sinfulness of the child. Others overemphasize the child's innocence and goodness. The former suggest lots of control and discipline from early in life. The latter emphasize treating the child well and making him feel good about himself. "Build up his self-esteem," they say, "and he will act in accord with the way he believes about himself."

We believe in three things. One, the child is created in the image of God and has a lot of good things about him from the start. He has many abilities and potentials God has passed on to the human race. Two, the child is a sinner. All of his goodness has been affected by sin, and he has an orientation that will rebel against truth, light, reality, and even love. And three, the child does not show up already assembled. He is immature and must be "put together" by the parenting process.

What this means is that everything a child does is not necessarily bad or good or immature. You have to discern which is which. For instance, if he cries, is he needy or manipulative? Some assume need makes a child cry; others assume selfishness. We believe that you must not assume anything, but learn to tell the difference and at what stages of growth it is more likely to be one than the other.

Some behavior may be the image of God manifesting itself. A child's exerting his will may be a very good thing and not disobedience or sin. If you break the will of a child, he may not have that will later to say no to drugs or sex. It is important to tell the difference between a good assertiveness, which you want to nurture, and rebellion, which you want to discipline, because your child is sure to test you with both.

Therefore, throughout this book you will find a balance reflecting this belief system. We want you to give to immature children who are in need and incomplete. We want you to discipline children who rebel against truth, you, God, and structure. We want you to nurture the very potential God built into them.

The Value of Freedom

Some parents believe in control. Others believe in permissiveness. Still others struggle to balance the two. We believe that God created humankind to grow into self-control (Galatians 5:23). So we will not help you to just gain control of your kids. We will not help your children get you off their backs, either. We will help you to play a role that will help your children gain control of themselves and their own lives.

Therefore you will see a balance of freedom and responsibility throughout this book. We believe that freedom undergirds everything God has for people (Galatians 5:1). And that freedom is to be used responsibly in the service of love. Therefore freedom and responsibility must go hand in hand for a child to develop into a loving adult. We will help you to not fear the freedom of your children, but at the same time to require responsibility from them.

Thus, you will not raise little robots. You will help your children grow into free people who have learned how to use their freedom to choose good things—things like love, responsibility, service, and accomplishment.

The Role of God

Earlier we said that a person's character guides her through life (Psalm 25:21). But character is never complete without an understanding of who one is before God. A person who acts as if she *is God* is a person no one wants to be around for long.

Healthy people have the ability to see who God is, to love him, to obey him, and to take their proper role under him.

Parenting is the way God designed this process to begin. He gave parents the assignment to bring up children to understand him and to take their proper place before him. He saw this as the ultimate protection and promise (Deuteronomy 6:20–25). We want to help you to help your children to understand God and his values and their role before him. We also want to help you to help your children to understand his love and his ways. This will be a thread throughout the book as well.

The Process

Parenting is a process that begins with conception and ends many years later. Some might say, "Once a parent, always a parent," or "You never cross the finish line in parenting." However, your parenting role does change. As the Bible says, the guardian and manager roles end one day (Galatians 4:2).

You will not get your parenting role right all at once, nor is there one thing you are supposed to get right. What needs to be done changes every day. Once you understand the principles involved, you will be more likely to go along for the ride, doing the right thing and enjoying the trip.

Some parenting experts emphasize that if you do certain things, your child will turn out right. But, there are no guarantees that children will turn out right because children have free will. You are responsible for the process, but God is in charge of the results. We have written this book to help you with the process.

We have not organized the book chronologically. Although we have plenty of age-specific guidelines in the book, we wanted you to be adequately equipped with the necessary ingredient at whatever parenting juncture you find yourself. We have written this book with a focus on the necessary ingredients and tasks, no matter what your child's age. Where age-specific interventions are needed, we have provided you with maps and instructions. But most important, we want you to have guidelines no matter where you find yourself in the process, from infancy to college. The MOPS team has assisted us in reviewing the manuscript twice and making helpful suggestions.

One difficult reality about parenting is that many of you reading this book are doing it solo as a single parent. This can be a great hardship on you, for parenting has so many demands that God designed it to be a partnership with another person. You may wonder if this material applies to your situation. We want you to know that we designed it with all parents in mind, both married and single. God's principles of child rearing are universal. In addition, however, we also added a chapter on single parenting for special situations that you particularly may need to address with your child.

Godspeed

We believe that parents desperately want to raise great kids. Parents want to do the right thing, and they can, given the right help. We hope you will find this book to be one of the many helps you will need along the way. If you find it to balance the role of love with the need for limits, we have written clearly. If you find it to value the worth of children without turning them into little gods, we have communicated what we believe. If you find it to say that children have much potential but need a lot of both nurturing and correction to achieve that, we have said what we wanted to say.

To give you additional specific help, we are planning three workbooks for parents to accompany this book: one for parents of preschoolers (0–5), another for parents of school-age children (6–12), and a third for parents of teenagers (13–19).

Ultimately, we believe in God's plan for parenting as outlined in the principles of the Bible. We don't believe in a particular, rigid way of following those principles. But we strongly believe that if you violate any of his principles, both you and your child will pay, and probably some other people as well. Therefore, do not get hung up on the specific "how to's." If a time-out in a chair, for example, is not good for your child, some other form of consequence will be. What is important is that discipline exists.

Pray hard, get lots of support, implement what we suggest, and enjoy the trip. May God be with you each and every step along the way. And, let's raise some great kids!

Part One

Raising Children of Character

——— One ———

The Goal of Parenting

A Child with Character

My friend Tony had asked me (Dr. Townsend) to dinner to talk about a family problem. After we caught up on what was new in our lives since we had last seen each other, he began talking about his recent struggles with his fourteen-year-old daughter, Halley. She was skipping school, drinking, and hanging around with a bad crowd. Tony and his wife, Denise, were working with the school, their church, and a counselor to deal with Halley's behavior.

"It must be awful. How are you handling it?" I asked Tony.

"It's been tough for all of us," Tony said. "But for me the worst part is what we've lost."

"What do you mean?"

"Remember when Halley was three or four?"

I nodded, having been friends with the family for years.

"She was the sweetest, most responsive kid you'd ever see," he said. "We were all so close. Halley wasn't perfect, but she was a good girl. Then out of the blue, this angry, lying, rebellious person seems to inhabit my daughter's body. I don't know this Halley."

I sat quietly with my friend, empathizing with his sense of loss.

Sometime later, Tony and I met again, and I asked about Halley. With a look of weary wisdom, he said, "We've all worked hard, and things are a lot better. I've learned some things about how we raised Halley. We wanted her to be *good.* But we weren't doing a lot about helping her *have good character.* That's our focus nowadays."

Tony's observation illustrates an important point about parenting. Everybody wants good kids. Good children do what they're supposed to. This is a proper and right desire. We are all to do what is good and right in God's eyes (Deuteronomy 12:28). But many good children don't grow up handling life well. They may become either not-so-good people or good-but-immature adults.

As Tony learned, the issue is not about being good, but about having good character. That is the subject of this chapter.

The Importance of Being a Parent

If you are a parent, congratulations! You are engaged in one of the most meaningful jobs in the world. Although cleaning up spilled milk and arguing about dirty rooms may seem trivial, you are doing eternally significant work: developing a little person into an adult.

God understands and supports you in this endeavor. People didn't invent parenting, God did. He is in a parent-child role with us, his people, forever. He loves us and wants to nurture and develop us. He wants us to call him by a parent name: "Father."

Being a parent is one of the most important tasks God gives anyone. Children are a blessing and a great heritage. Through parenting, humanity continues down through the centuries, our spiritual and cultural values are preserved, and the image of God is revealed in every new generation.

Parenting is a huge task. Parents shoulder the burden of being the source of life, love, and growth for their children. One of the elements of childhood is *dependency*. Dependency defines a child. Children look to and need parents for all those things they can't provide for themselves. Especially in the early years, the parent takes responsibility for both knowing and giving needed elements of life to the child. A dependent person (child) and a source person (parent) are at the core of the parent-child relationship.

If you are reading this book, most likely you willingly chose the responsibility of becoming a parent. If this isn't true, you have certainly still accepted this responsibility. Most parents have strong values and emotions that influence them to raise kids. For example, they want to:

Create love with a spouse, which can transfer down to another generation

Pass on their values to others

Create a warm and caring family context

Have fun with their kids

Contribute something to the world

These are all good reasons for parenting. However, once you have become a parent, it can be hard to get your head above water long enough to figure out exactly what you are trying to accomplish and how you will know when you get there. Parents need a way to keep in mind the ultimate goal of parenting.

Creating an Adult

Most parents want their children to grow up. In other words, we define success not by how our children are doing today, but by what happens after they leave home. Imagine your children as adults in the following areas of life:

School. They are investing in training for life and career.

Job. They are growing in career life.

Dating. They are choosing people who are mature and have good values.

Marriage. They have chosen a life's partner, and they are working at their marriage.

Friendships. They have a close-knit group of friends who support them.

Personal values and conduct. They have thought through what is important to them and live consistently with good values.

Spiritual life. They are actively involved in a relationship with God.

All these help define what is a functioning adult. Adults take on the challenges of life and find their niche. They know what is important to them, and they focus on those things. They know their limits, and what they can't provide for themselves they are able to get from outside resources.

God designed your child to function independently of you. This is what is so difficult about parenting: It's the only relationship designed by God that measures success by how well it ends. You are investing in helping your child leave you. In the biblical teaching that children should leave father and mother (Genesis 2:24), the meaning of *leave* is "to forsake." Every mom and dad who have sacrificed for and loved a child suffer a real parent-wound when their child grows up and leaves. And yet mature parents gladly suffer this wound, because they know the benefits the child will receive from their investment.

Sadly, kids don't always grow up well. Sometimes they don't leave, and they depend on their parents far too long. At other times they leave, but they aren't prepared for adult life. They may not depend on their parents any longer, but they aren't functioning well in love or work. They are adults on the outside, but they are broken or undeveloped on the inside.

Who Is Responsible for What?

Who is responsible for your child's maturity and readiness for the world—you or your child? This important question deeply affects a parent's attitude toward a child. Answers to it fall on opposite ends of the spectrum. Some see the child's successes or failures in life as primarily the parent's responsibility. These parents diligently do whatever they can to help their child grow, and they feel that the child's adult years reflect on how they parented. Others see the child as taking the weight. "I did my best, and he had a choice," they say when problems arise.

We believe in the following three principles about responsibility.

1. Responsibility lies on a continuum between child and parent, and where it lies on the continuum changes over time. The child's only responsibility at the beginning of life is to need and take in the sources of life; parents have total responsibility for

the child. As the child begins to assert himself, learn tasks, and become more self-sufficient, he takes more ownership of his life and the parent takes less. Around the beginning of the teen years, the parent actively begins "de-parenting," that is, exchanging a controlling role in the child's life for an influential one. By the time he reaches the late teens, the child should be taking over total responsibility for his behavior, finances, morality, and relationships.

2. Even though responsibility shifts, both parents and children still have their own unique and distinct tasks. Parents provide safety and love, and they also structure experiences to help the child mature. The child responds to these experiences, takes risks, fails, and learns lessons. Parents and children can't do each other's jobs; they must do their own. Parents who ask their child if it's okay to be a parent are in trouble. The question, "Is it all right with you if I set a curfew?" does not show parental authority. And the child who tries to take responsibility for her parents' feelings also has a problem.

3. The child must bear the ultimate responsibility for his life. No parent is perfect, and all children suffer some injuries along with the benefits they receive from their parents. Early childhood experiences are life-changing. In major ways they determine the kind of adults children grow up to be. Yet, in the end, a child will be evaluated not as much on his circumstances and environment, but on how he responded to what life handed out: Did he love? Did he practice stewardship? Did he grow, change, and forgive?

The Bible says that at the end of life we will all be called to account for the good and bad we did in life (2 Corinthians 5:10). While your child is coming to terms today with what his tasks are and are not, he always needs to be moving toward full responsibility for his life and soul.

Your Parenting Reflects Your Goals

Ironically, we often know our financial and career goals more clearly than we do our child-rearing goals. One difficulty with setting parenting goals is that kids have their own say-so and may have different ideas. In addition, parenting is so demanding that it's hard to take a long-term view. You have many fires to put out, and today's worries keep you busy enough.

Yet, if someone said to you, "What is the goal of your parenting?" you might identify with some of the following approaches.

Survival. Keep things on an even keel from day to day. A financial or marital struggle, for example, may keep parents in crisis. Their goal is making it to the next day. As you would expect, the child's welfare often suffers with this approach.

Independence. Teach children to be self-sufficient. "If I can just get them grown up and living on their own, I'll settle for that," a battle-worn mom or dad might say of a teen. Teaching a child self-sufficiency has a lot of merit, yet many adults can work and support themselves but have large problems in other areas such as making friends or finding a life's partner.

Competence. Teach children to be competent. This is the hallmark of our era. To provide their children with a good background, "soccer moms and dads" exhaust themselves with sports, arts activities, and social events. Every Saturday is dedicated to a kid's games and tournaments. While kids learn valuable skills, teamwork, and socialization, they may miss out on other areas of life such as intimacy, home responsibilities, and spiritual values.

Problem Solving. Address problems as they come up. Parents work on behavioral problems, school issues, and attitude struggles. Good parents do face thousands of problems, yet some problems often hide deeper issues. An underachieving child, for example, may have developmental or family conflicts. He may be emotionally or cognitively immature. Or, he may be suffering from depression over the marriage problems of his parents. Problem solvers need to have overarching values and principles to guide them.

Morality. Teach children to be good. This was Tony's goal. He wanted his daughter Halley to grow up to be a "good person," a young woman who is pure and has good values. Yet morality is a complex attribute, as we will see later. A goal of morality alone may lead to problems with guilt, judgmentalism, or acting out.

Religious life. Most parents want God to be the center of their children's lives. We want kids who love God and follow his ways. Yet religious training that doesn't recognize the spiritual aspects of helping kids live real life is a weak goal. Many are the parents whose hearts were broken because their child learned the words of the Bible, but did not believe them in his heart or live them out in his life.

Character: The Real Goal

My friend Tony wanted his daughter to be a good kid. Good kids are a product of the real goal of parenting: *mature character.* When children grow up with mature character, they are able to take their place as adults in the world and function properly in all areas of life. Character growth is the main goal of child rearing.

But what is character? For some, the word *character* brings to mind pictures of a person who has integrity, takes responsibility for her life, and stands up for the right thing. Others may see character as the child's personality—those attributes that make her unique, such as energy level, interests, and a sense of humor. Personality is a child's emotional fingerprint—there's only one like it.

People with mature character do have traits of integrity, responsibility, and courage, but we understand character in a bigger-picture way. We view character as the structures and abilities within ourselves that make up how we operate in life. In other words, character is *the sum of our abilities to deal with life as God designed us to.* Reality makes certain demands on us, for example, to relate to other people in good ways, to do what we say we will do, to take ownership of our own mistakes, and to solve our own problems. Our success (or failure) in meeting these demands shows our level of character development.

You may know adults who look good and perform well but have character flaws. These character flaws—a bad temper, a tendency to withdraw, or self-centeredness—rear their ugly heads over and over again to diminish that person's life experience. More often than not, these flaws began in childhood and continued on in adulthood. This is why parenting is so critical; childhood is the time when character strengths and weaknesses are laid down. We are not telling you this to scare you, but simply to point out a truth. You can make great strides in helping your child be a person of character, or you can also miss its importance and see its effects in painful ways later in life. Better the first than the second. As the Bible teaches, make the most of your opportunities because the days are evil (Ephesians 5:16).

Randall found out early in life that if he failed, his guilt-ridden parents would buy just about any excuse he made for his failure. They didn't want to be mean or harsh with their son. So when he brought home conduct reports and bad grades from school, Randall would complain to his folks about that unfair teacher who had it in for him. Then Mom and Dad would march to the principal's office to straighten out the bad teacher.

Randall developed a character weakness in the area of personal responsibility. By the time he was in high school, he was an underachiever who blamed every problem on his environment, his lot in life, his circumstances, or his parents. His lack of character development was extremely costly to him. His underachievement caused him to lose friends, academic goals, and sports opportunities.

When you help your child develop character, you are addressing the heart of parenting. Character provides a tool kit of spiritual and emotional skills that prepare a child to succeed in life. You can give children all the "advantages"—security, good schools, churches, and camps—but if they don't develop character, they can quickly lose the advantage of the advantages. There are so many stories of children who had it all and squandered it. Or children who didn't have the character strength to meet life's rigors and broke down at some level in their career, their marriage, or their own parenting. Or those who had many talents and gifts, but ended up falling far short of the mark.

The Aspects of Character

What does character in a child look like? We will explain in detail in Part 2 the six distinct aspects of character. This explanation forms the heart of this book. But we will briefly introduce each aspect here. As you look at the list below, think about your child in each area. No matter what his age, he has character development tasks to do in each aspect that can help him grow to maturity.

Attachment. The most basic and important character ability is the ability to form relationships. Life comes from connectedness. Attachment to God and others is the source of all good things. Children need to learn to need, trust, depend, and have empathy for others. When your child falls down and skins her knee, your comfort helps her to experience and learn the value of reaching out.

Responsibility. Your child is born thinking her life is your problem. During the beginning of life, this is true. But part of growing character is helping her to take ownership over her life and to see her life as *her* problem. As she takes responsibility over her choices, she gradually experiences freedom and self-control.

Reality. This character trait deals with the ability of your child to accept the negatives of the real world. Her friends (and parents) will let her down. She herself will let others down. You will need to assist her in the process of dealing with sin, loss, failure, and evil, not only in herself, but in others and in the world.

Competence. Children need training to develop their God-given gifts and talents. They need to develop their skill not only in specialty areas such as art, sports, or science, but also in everyday matters, such as decision making, judgment, and work ethics.

Conscience. An internal sense of right and wrong is a growth process in children. Kids' consciences are developed at different ages and stages in life.

Worship. Your child has been created in the image of God. Certain tasks foster character development in spiritual growth. For example, children need to learn that God loves them and is in charge of life. They also need to learn to seek God on their own, apart from their parents.

When you see this analysis of character, you may have several reactions. You may be overwhelmed with the size and complexity of the child-rearing task. You may be relieved that there is a structure to help you organize your parenting. You may be discouraged with a problem area or two. Or you may even be thinking about your own character issues. Actually, all of these responses make sense.

It's important to note here that these character aspects are attributes of God's own character. God attaches and loves (John 3:16). God takes responsible ownership of his life (Psalm 64:9). God lives in reality (Psalm 10:14). God is expert in all he does (Genesis 1:31). God is the only one qualified to handle good and evil (Genesis 3:22). And God lives in the eternal (Revelation 4:9–10).

The difference is that while God has always had these character traits, your child is in the process of developing them. She may have been born with a certain unique temperament, such as a tendency to be more introspective or more active. But she wasn't born with mature character. Your first, last, and best goal is to be a good agent of developing this within her life and soul.

How Character Is Developed

Growing your child's character always involves two elements: *development,* or training through experience and practice; and *internalizing,* or taking those experiences inside to become a part of his personality. We will deal with these two elements in more detail in the next chapter. However, here we would like to explain the difference between teaching and experience in your parenting.

Teaching transfers information from one to another. But teaching alone doesn't make the child "own," or take responsibility for, the information. The Bible mentions two types of "knowing": we are to "know" (or understand) the truth to be free (John 8:32), and Adam "knew" (or experienced in an intimate personal way) Eve (Genesis 4:1 KJV). Your child needs not only to understand relationship, responsibility, and goal setting, but also to experience these realities in an intimate, personal way.

The operative word for this part of character development is *experience*. The Bible itself uses the word *experience* to explain character (Romans 5:4 KJV). In other words, we grow from what we engage in. For example, you can't learn how to ride a bicycle from just reading a book; you have to get on a bike. In the same way, character parenting provides a wealth of experiences that help the child learn about realities such as relationship, responsibility, and forgiveness.

Think of some activity you love and have mastered. Perhaps it is making scrapbooks or playing golf or playing the guitar. Remember how bad you were when you were starting the activity. You looked like a beginner, because you were. You had a hard time with the basics. The activity didn't feel natural. Then, after a while, it became a part of you, and now it's second nature; in fact, you may be at an advanced level, helping others enjoy your passion.

What made the difference between being a beginner and wherever you are now? You invested a lot of energy in some training experiences over a period of time. You didn't will yourself into being an expert overnight. Small tasks, repeated in many ways, with lots of failures, caused you to learn.

This is how character is developed in kids. Your child needs to be actively engaged in maturing at all stages of life. He starts out as a mistrustful, irresponsible, self-centered being—a beginner in character. And as you give him character-training experiences over time, his abilities to connect, take responsibility, and give to others gradually increase and expand. In fact, if the process goes as it was designed, your child will stay on the journey of character growth long after he has left home, all the way through life.

Many parents have difficulty with this concept. Although we have lots of evidence to prove otherwise, we still think that if we tell kids to do the right thing enough times, they'll turn around and do it!

One time I was coaching Little League for seven-year-old boys. When our team was at bat, my job was to keep order in the dugout. The goal was to have the kids sit quietly next to each other on the bench, cheer their buddies who were hitting, and pay attention to the nuances of the game.

What would really happen is that the guys would poke each other, grab and toss each others' hats, and jump around. I would say, "Guys! Pay attention! Shhh!" This was teaching at its finest: information with no experience. And it was profoundly ineffectual. Telling ten boys to be quiet a hundred times is an exercise in futility.

By the end of the season, I was sick of keeping order, though I loved the other aspects of coaching.

Then my wife returned from a game she attended and raved about a coach who had her dugout kids in perfect form. They were quiet and attentive. Her secret, Barbi told me, was that she had a chart that measured the boys' behavior in sitting still, noise level, and other things. The ones who were doing well were earning tokens for a snack. The others were being sent around the field to run laps and were losing turns at bat. This might seem like the Marines to some, but none of the kids' parents were complaining. They could finally watch a game without distraction.

Experience made the difference. The kids' coach provided experiences of sitting still, keeping their hands off their friends' bodies and hats, and cheering for their teammates who were at bat and on base, and she provided rewards for good behavior and consequences for misbehavior. The kids began changing and responding to these rewards and consequences.

While it's important to teach your child about loving and being loved, and about taking responsibility (Deuteronomy 6:20–25), information is never enough. Your child needs many, many experiences in which he sees reality and adapts to it, or suffers the consequences of ignoring it.

How to Know What to Develop

It is easy to be overwhelmed by the complexity of character development. You must deal with several character aspects of your child at once; you don't have the option of working on one issue until it is resolved, then moving to the next. Your child needs to be growing in each area continuously, but with different tasks and levels of maturity as he grows.

For example, in the area of reality, a three-year-old is working on understanding that the people who gratify him are the same ones who frustrate him. He needs to discover the reality that the world isn't divided into good people and bad people, but is full of people who are both good and bad. When this child is thirteen, however, he will struggle with his own overconfidence in his abilities versus his constant failure in learning how to relate to his parents and the opposite sex. The same character aspect has different goals for the child at different ages.

You will need to learn to develop awareness for your child in these areas. When you drive a car, you constantly check the windshield, rearview mirror, speedometer, and steering wheel. In the same way, you want to monitor where your child is in his relational abilities, his sense of responsibility, and his ability to deal with loss, for example. Certain developmental stages major on some specific aspects more than others. For example, infancy is a time of almost exclusive attachment and bonding. It is such a demanding job and the infant is so young, there is not time for much else.

This book will provide a road map for you to evaluate where your child is in the major character areas. Character development is designed to proceed at a fairly predictable rate over time. However, factors such as interactions with parents, the child's choices, and external circumstances sometimes result in some character aspects developing at different paces than others. A little boy may relate to others successfully early in life, but have problems controlling his behavior. Then, a few years later, there can be a reversal, in which he has succeeded in controlling his behavior, but is having people conflicts.

Or a child may consistently struggle in one area throughout her youth. From early childhood to adolescence, she may have a harsh conscience that condemns her for failures, rather than providing her with reality about her actions. Parents need to be aware of this long-term issue to help her resolve it before the onset of adulthood.

Fruits and Roots

When you understand and interact with your child on a character level, you will quickly find that what seems to be a problem isn't really *the* problem. Character has to do with the way the child sees and acts in the world. You can't see or touch character; to use computer technology, it is being hard-wired inside your child's brain. What you can see is how he responds to life.

Your child's behavior, attitudes, and emotions serve as an indicator light about character issues. By observing, you will know better how to provide growth experiences tailored to help your child mature and develop in a particular area.

Jesus taught this principle in terms of fruits: "Every good tree bears good fruit, but a bad tree bears bad fruit" (Matthew 7:17). Just as you can understand the nature of the tree from its fruit, you can understand the character of your child from her actions. Then, if a problem arises, you deal with the root of the issue, not its symptom.

My friend Amanda's second-grade daughter, Pat, was constantly reporting that her two best friends were being unkind, ignoring her, and making fun of her. Several days a week she would come crying to her mom's car after school.

Amanda realized the problem wasn't a "bad friends" problem; it was a "demanding Pat" problem. Pat's friends couldn't be free and be in relationship with her. This was a signal to Amanda to help Pat with some character work. They began talking about it. What was especially helpful was that Amanda stopped siding with Pat against the girlfriends and instead gently explained that friends have to let friends make their own choices. This forced Pat out of her victim stance and helped her see her own part in the problem.

"Fruit" problems—such as biting, throwing tantrums, and sulking—can be alarming, demanding, and frustrating. And you certainly need to set limits with and consequences on the behaviors themselves. But don't stop there. Effective parents look for what a symptom is showing them about their child's struggle to grow up, and they deal with helping her on that level.

Now that you have the big-picture goal of parenting as character building, the next two chapters will explain the ingredients God has provided that produce growth in children: grace, truth, and time.

Two

The Ingredients of Grace and Truth

Karen and Dan were discussing their twelve-year-old son, Jason. They had had similar discussions many times. The topic this time was about his schoolwork.

"He must learn that things do not come easy in life. I come home day after day, and he has not even thought about doing his homework," Dan said.

"I know, honey," Karen said, "but he's only twelve. He's small for his age and has trouble feeling secure around other kids. We just need to encourage him now. He needs to feel good about himself, not just get ragged on about not doing 'good enough.'"

"What do you mean 'ragged on'? Do you think that's what I'm doing? I'm trying to help him get ahead. When I was his age, I had a paper route, played sports, and still made good grades."

"Yes, I know. But you were different. He's not the driver type. He's more sensitive and needs to be built up to feel good about himself. I am worried about his self-esteem."

"Self-esteem! What are you talking about? You need to forget all that psychobabble. He's never going to feel good about himself until he starts performing. He's becoming a loser, and you are just letting him skate by." Dan was getting frustrated. He always felt that Karen was too lenient on the children, especially Jason.

"There you go again, calling him a loser. He'll never be able to do well if you make him feel like he's so bad."

"I'm not making him feel bad by wanting a little discipline in his life. Every day he comes home, plays all day, gets whatever he wants, and you just let him do it."

"I do not. I just don't think that he needs to hear so much about how he always needs to do better. Kids do well when they're encouraged, not told where they're failing. Don't you remember how your father made you feel?"

"My father may have been tough, but that did me a lot of good," Dan said. "Look where I am today! This didn't come from just getting milk and cookies every time things got tough. Kids need their fannies pushed if they are ever going to turn into anything." Then he pulled out the heavy artillery. "The Bible says that we have to understand God's standards and learn to live up to them. You never make him face the truth, and it's spoiling him rotten. We said that we were going to raise a godly child this time, remember?"

Dan was referring to the rearing of their older child, Benjamin, whom they had raised before they had become Christians. Benjamin had had problems in the teen years and afterward, and both Dan and Karen vowed that they would parent Jason according to biblical principles. "The truth is good for him. Better that he learn to face it now than later!"

"But that is not all the Bible says," Karen came back. "It says that we need grace and compassion. You are so hard on him when he doesn't meet your expectations. How is he ever going to understand the grace of God if all we do is make him feel guilty?"

Dan shook his head, sighed, and walked away. Karen went and offered Jason some ice cream. Dan and Karen did not feel very close the rest of the evening.

Grace and Truth Divided

Does this conversation sound familiar? Maybe you and your spouse do not get as heated as did Dan and Karen. But you frequently find yourselves on different sides of the argument when you need to decide between "cutting some slack" or enforcing the limits. Or, even more commonly, maybe you do not find yourself at odds with your spouse, but discover you are at odds with yourself on this issue. You find yourself being lenient for a season, only to finally get frustrated and angrily "lower the boom." Your child may look up at you wondering, "Where did you come from?" Sometimes you are nice but a pushover, and sometimes you are stern and not very nice at all.

Who was right, Dan or Karen? Or which self should you be, the nice one or the strict one? Parents have been divided over this question for centuries, often with the result of either having confused kids or having one child who is too hard on himself while his sister is totally freewheeling and irresponsible.

The problem is that the very ingredients we need for growth—grace and truth—are divided against one another. Choosing between the two is not the problem. Getting them together is. We tend to practice one or the other in a given moment or season, or with a particular person. An effective parent must learn to be gracious and truthful at the same time.

First, let's define the two ingredients.

Grace, in the Bible's terms, means "favor." Grace-filled people are kind toward others; they are "for" a person and not against him. Usually this favor is spoken of as "unmerited." In other words, true grace is not earned; it is given freely out of love. Grace shows itself in many forms and qualities:

- Kindness
- Empathy
- Forgiveness
- Compassion
- Understanding
- Provision
- Love
- Help

Truth is the state of being reliable and trustworthy. It is ultimately reality, the timeless realities God wove into his creation. If we live in truth, we do what is right. In addition, a truthful person is someone who faces what "really is." Truth shows itself in the Bible in many forms:

- Morality
- Standards
- Expectations

- Evaluations
- Judgment
- Confrontation
- Discipline
- Limits
- Honesty
- Integrity

Any parent would agree that both groups are important.

Problems arise when the two ingredients get divided, when we practice one without the other. In the above example, Karen was very aware of the need to show grace to her son, giving him kindness and compassion, understanding his difficulty fitting in with the other kids. She wanted him to know that he was loved and accepted just the way he was, unconditionally, so that he would not be insecure in her or God's love.

But in her concern for showing him grace, she was leaving out truth. He did not have a standard before him that he was required to live up to." He was getting "love without limits." Dan was going to give Jason the missing ingredient. He felt intuitively that his child needed more structure, discipline, and limits. And he provided these when he was there.

The problem was that just as Karen gave love without limits, Dan was often guilty of giving limits without love. He would be harsh, focusing only on the rules and where Jason stood in relation to them. As a result, Jason was feeling estranged from Dan and afraid of him and his harshness.

What will happen to Jason? It's too early to tell, but research, the Bible, and experience point to a few predictable patterns in children raised with grace and truth divided. If a child sides with one parent over the other, he adopts a style that identifies with what this parent was to him. For example, if Jason identifies more with his mom, he will probably lean toward letting himself slide when requirements are upon him. Inside, he will have internalized a loving mother's voice saying, "That's okay, Jason. Everything is still okay, even if you did not do what you were supposed to." But this ignores reality. It is not okay to just slide. The night before a final exam in college he will accept the invitation to go out and party, ignoring the reality that he should study.

If he sides more with his father, he could be under the demands of a critical conscience, never able to do enough and always threatening himself with guilt, fear, and maybe even anger at his imperfections. He would never accept an invitation to a party, even early in the semester, because he would always have to study.

If he were aggressive, he might rebel against his dad's harshness. The Bible warns us of this possibility when Paul says, "Do not provoke your children to anger" (Ephesians 6:4 NASB). Or, like most of us, Jason would probably internalize both sides of grace and truth and struggle with getting them together himself. At times, he would let himself slide and then get harsh with himself when he ultimately failed to measure up. Most of us can identify with some aspect of feeling divided between grace and truth.

Integration

One goal of parenting is to integrate grace and truth. From the earliest days on, parents must at the same time love their child and provide limits and structure. They must be loving and firm. They must be kind, but require the child to do his part. They must be compassionate and forgiving, but require the child to change and be responsible. Soft on the person, but hard on the issue.

What does this look like? Remember this formula:

Grace establishes and maintains the quality of the relationship, and truth adds direction for the growth and structure of a child's behavior and performance. Grace lets a child know she is loved. Truth guides her on what to do and become.

Parents who have integrated grace and truth give messages that contain both:

"I know you want to play now. It's hard to wait. But I want you to finish your homework first, and then you can play.

"I forgive you for what you did. But if you do it again, you
    will be grounded for a day."
"I'm on your side, even if you don't feel it. But you are
    going to have to respect the rules, too."

Dan and Karen talked to a friend who helped them see their
extremes. As Dan began to integrate grace into the truth he had
provided, he became more loving in his discipline of Jason. He
empathized with Jason's fears of failure, his difficulty with staying on task, and his feeling of smallness in the world of other
children. He nurtured Jason when Jason did not obey, saying
things like, "I know it is hard. I don't like to go to work sometimes either. But I'm pulling for you. Clean up your room, and
then we can shoot some hoops." This was a big change from
"Jason! Get back in here right now and get to work. I'm tired
of your lollygagging. You're so lazy!"

And Karen began to integrate truth into the grace she had
provided. She added some requirements and structure to Jason's
day. She held off on granting Jason permission to do what he
wanted until he did what was required. She even learned to
enforce disciplinary consequences.

Same Formula, Different Content

As children grow, your expression of grace and truth needs
to change. At different ages, children need different kinds of
kindness and structure. But the formula is the same: Grace and
truth must go together. In the following chart are some illustrations of how grace and truth have different content at different ages:

STAGE	GRACE	TRUTH
Infancy (First Year)	Understand an infant's total dependency. Give compassion and empathy liberally.	For the most part, you do not have to provide truth and structure. His being alone, uncomforted, hungry, separate, and totally dependent

	Feed and nurse when needed.	teaches an infant enough difficult truth for now.
	Soothe and comfort at the onset of distress.	As infants begin to get more into a natural routine in later months, gradually introduce the structure of feeding and nap times, allowing more frustration after needs are met.
Toddlerhood	Empathize with and understand the toddler's lack of maturity.	Introduce limits and boundaries, in having more space and structuring time. As they live out their freedom in that space, have limits on some behavior.
	Comfort when you discipline.	Introduce discipline and correction.
	Coach and guide a toddler's explorations.	Introduce language and the use of words.
	Understand the fear of a toddler separating and becoming more independent; do not require more than a toddler is able to tolerate.	Teach the toddler to respond to "No."
		Limit open rebellion and defiance lovingly.
	Reestablish the connection after discipline with assurances of love.	Require more separateness—for example, leave the toddler with a baby-sitter and require him to sleep alone.
		Limit tantrums and inappropriate expressions of aggression.
		Teach social skills, such as table manners, saying

		please and thank-you, and using the toilet.
Childhood Years (approx. 3-12)	Teach skills and provide opportunities to learn new things. Encourage learning new skills. Provide experiences. Understand failure and have patience. Show forgiveness. Grant freedoms and privileges that are earned.	Set rules that protect children from danger. Give requirements that teach more and more responsibility. Enforce consequences of disobedience or non-performance. Teach more advanced social skills, such as manners and kindness to others. Require children to take responsibility and to repent when wrong.
Adolescence	Empathize with and understand adolescents' need for dependency and their wish for autonomy. Forgive the natural limit testing and rule breaking. Give adolescents more latitude in determining preferences and choices. Understand adolescents' need to choose their own values. Grant more and more freedom when earned.	Provide clear limits and moral guidelines. Enforce consequences and loss of freedom when responsibility is not shown. Require adolescents to earn their way financially. Require them to manage their own time and resources. Limit inappropriate expressions of disrespect, aggression, and sexuality.

	Grant more resources and opportunities for independence and further skill building. Have compassion for the heartbreak and failure that adolescent insecurity and experience offer.	
College Age	Understand an adolescent's budding sexuality. Encourage and cheerlead. Offer guidance and some resources. Provide a safe place to process losses and difficulties. Give space to figure out direction and goals.	Have clear requirements on who pays for what. Set clear requirements on how your college-age child can keep your financial or other material support. Communicate honestly about how you think and feel about their choices. Give your opinions about what you think is good for them. Give them space to make their own choices and suffer the consequences. Do not intrude on the time management of their lives. Enforce limits regarding living with you. Make them share responsibility for the house, and so on.

		Enforce limits of legal and moral standards for people living in your house—e.g., you do not allow drugs in your home.

As you can see, the way that parents display grace and truth to a toddler is very different from the way they display it to a teenager. But the formula is the same. Both ingredients must be in the mix. Think of following the advice in only one of the columns, and then try to imagine what a child would feel like if grace or truth is all she receives from her parent (children have been known to ask for grace only!). Few parents would subscribe to one column only, but many parents end up operating out of one column, if only for a season. For a child to develop character, she needs to be given grace and truth in virtually every interaction.

Why These Two?

In all of the parenting literature throughout the ages, grace and truth stand out. One usually hears them referred to as "love and limits." Why? It goes all the way back to the creation of humankind. In the beginning, the Bible says, God created Adam in his image, or likeness. That means different things to different people. Theologians speak about capacities such as mind, will, emotion, and morality.

The Bible again and again describes God as a being of grace and truth, of compassion and truth, of mercy and righteousness. In fact, one psalm describes God as someone in whom these two qualities are merged: "Lovingkindness and truth have met together; righteousness and peace have kissed each other" (Psalm 85:10 NASB). In another psalm, King David sees his need for God to bring these ingredients to him in his time of need: "Do not withhold your mercy from me, O LORD; may your love and your truth always protect me" (Psalm 40:11).

As God lives out these qualities and passes them on to us as his creation, we are to live them out as well. We need to have the love that sustains our relationships in life and the truth that guides us to safety and good performance.

But there is a problem. We are not born with these qualities fully developed. We are only born with the *potential* for these qualities. For the potential to become reality, the qualities of grace and truth must be developed and internalized within us. We will talk more throughout the book about the twin constructs of *develop* and *internalize*. But a brief explanation will help put them into the context of grace and truth.

To develop means "to cause to grow or expand." Good parents help children to grow and expand their capacities for grace and truth. As we will see in the next chapter, this happens over time. But it cannot happen on its own. Parents are the chief agents in this process. As you love and discipline your children, set requirements and provide consequences, nurture and teach, and help them get through failure and turn it into learning, your children will grow through experience. The potential is there, but it has to be "grown and expanded." You as the parent are a big "cause" of the growth and expansion.

But children need more than experience and practice. They need to *internalize* grace and truth. They need to take inside of themselves what they see and experience in their primary relationships outside of themselves. As parents model grace and truth, children take these qualities into themselves as part of their personalities; grace and truth are forever etched into the hard-wiring of their brains to guide them through life. Grace and truth become the "voices" inside that encourage them through the day, help them feel a sense of hope, love, and forgiveness, and correct them when they do wrong and no one is looking over their shoulders. These qualities cause them to feel appropriate anxiety about the need to get jobs done, or the need not to violate conscience and standards, and they become the fuel to move them along that path.

I will never forget the first time I saw the effect of harsh truth without grace internalized in a child. Kelly was five years old when I began working with her. She had been taken from a foster home for disruptive behavior and social withdrawal. When she came into my office, she seemed very pleasant. We began to play shortly thereafter. But in the course of play, Kelly dropped her toy. She immediately began to berate herself, saying, "Stupid girl! Stupid girl!" It was difficult to stop her. Kelly had internalized the harsh confrontations she had received.

Not long after that, I was at a friend's house. His four-year-old daughter, who was playing on the floor, knocked over her dad's Coke. Instantly her eyes widened, and she exclaimed, "Oops! That's okay." She then righted the can and went to get some paper towels to clean up the spill. She automatically displayed what she had heard when she had made other mistakes. She saw the mistake, but she had experienced grace. What she had heard and experienced in her family had become a part of her.

The maxim is this: *What was once outside becomes inside.* If a child hears soothing, forgiving, encouraging voices, and if she experiences these in her relationships, she will have these qualities as part of her makeup, and they will guide her through life. If she receives correction, discipline, instruction, truthful confrontation, and consequences, she will have the truth and reality that will guide her to perform along those lines. But she will not be able to put them together if she has not experienced them together.

Give children grace and give them truth. But don't give one without the other. Let them discover that reality, the truth, is actually *for* them and not *against* them. Ultimately, that is what the two do. Grace shows them favor, that someone is for them and on their team. Truth shows them *that reality is real and how to live it*. Give them both.

Grace and truth are both ingredients in raising great kids. But you need one more ingredient, which we will discuss in the next chapter.

——— Three ———

The Ingredient of Time

When I (Dr. Cloud) graduated from high school, the local newspaper decided to take a special photo. The press had taken all the normal pictures of the class valedictorian and the honor students and the members of various service groups, clubs, and organizations. But on this particular occasion, they included another picture. So many students from our high school were granted athletic scholarships and were invited to join major university teams that the press took a group photo of the fifteen or twenty students from our school who were going on to play NCAA sports.

Later, as I looked at this photo, I noticed that many of these athletes had been together since elementary school. Then it hit me: one coach had started all these athletes on their path to success. His name was Kayo Dottley.

When we were in elementary school, Kayo coached our football team—the Bowmar Greyhounds. A retired NFL running back, he had set many records in his own illustrious college career. But after a knee injury finished his career in his first year with the Chicago Bears, he moved back to Mississippi to raise a family and go into business. Loving sports and children as he did, Kayo decided to coach his two sons' Little League football teams.

But Kayo was not your normal Little League coach. Whereas most coaches spent a little time once or twice a week with their teams, Kayo knew you could not be world champions with such little practice time. We practiced every day. Every day after school, Kayo would organize forty or so very little football players into scrimmage squads and drill teams.

And then, for three hours or so a day, we would work. We would do blocking drills, tackling drills, pass routines, offense coordination, defense configurations—and everything else a professional team did. We were so organized that colleges could have taken lessons from us. Every day Kayo and his assistant coaches (friends who also had sons playing) would teach, correct, challenge, encourage, scold, and yell us into shape. Hour after hour, drill after drill. Do it once, hear what you did wrong, do it again.

It was amazing! Parents would come to watch with glee as they saw their sons develop in ability and character.

Every year for five years—the length of time Kayo Dottley coached—the Bowmar Greyhounds won the city championship. For five years we went undefeated. And for Kayo's entire last year (and if I remember correctly other years as well), no team ever scored against us until a fullback from another team illegally crawled over the goal line and the referees let it stand because the rest of the city was so happy someone else had finally scored a point. In the end, parents signed a petition to have Kayo forced out of the league so other teams would have a chance to win.

But that day, twelve years later, when I saw the picture of so many young men headed off to college careers, I had to smile. The time Kayo had spent with us was still bearing fruit. Hundreds of hours of character training—not to mention thousands of dollars in scholarships—would last these young men a lifetime, all because one man gave of his time in a way that helped children grow. Kayo gave us the grace of his encouragement and the truth of his knowledge and correction, but he mixed them with time to build the skills and character we would need for later success.

Let's take a look at some of the ways the ingredient of time works for a growing child.

The Nature and Importance of Time

In chapter 2 we talked about the ingredients of grace and truth and the processes of development and internalization. Grace and truth could be given in an instant, but for children to grow, parents must give these two ingredients over and over again in a process that follows children down prescribed developmental lines God has wired into them. Maturity develops as parents or caretakers, through countless interactions, match their children's time-sensitive needs of who they are with the right kind of interaction from the outside world along a very predictable process.

In this chapter we want to look at how the following three elements of time are involved in the development of a child:

1. Quantity of time
2. The way the process works
3. The God-given developmental path

We have all heard about the importance of giving time to your children. Quantity is the foundation. You cannot grow children on just "quality time." Growing children, first of all, takes quantities of time. But even lots of time is not enough. We all know people who spend a lot of time with their children and still have significant problems. That is because the time must, secondly, be spent in a particular way. It must be structured in a certain way with certain things happening. And thirdly, children have a God-given agenda of how they will use the moments you give to them. They have a developmental path. So let's look at how all three aspects of time relate to your child.

More Time, Please

The story of Kayo shows us the importance of quantities of time. He gave much more than one expects from a volunteer coach. But he was not just volunteering to coach a bunch of kids. He was giving time to his two sons. The rest of us were just beneficiaries of the love and care he was giving to his children. With all of this time, we were able to develop the skills needed.

Can you imagine playing that first game without having had time to practice? What if Kayo had believed that all you need is "quality time"? What if he had just spent an hour or so of quality time every few weeks trying to teach us the game? This would have never done it.

Why not? Why does quality not do it alone? Why do we need quantity?

First of all, children are living organisms, like plants. They are growing. The very tense of that verb implies something ongoing, not static. Growth is happening all the time in a continuous process. So, if children are growing, someone had better be sure that this growth is happening in the right direction.

For example, if you plant a vine in your yard, it will grow. It is living. Where it will grow and what direction it takes, as well as the health of the vine, is totally up to you. If you ignore it, growth will happen, but probably in the wrong direction and without the proper sustenance. You may get a call from your neighbor saying, "Your vine is taking over my yard. It choked my plumbing, and you owe me some money." Or he might say, "That vine has a fungus that has infected all my rose bushes. My lawyer will be calling you."

Yes, children will grow. But without you, they will go their own way. Your children could end up being trespassers, going into places where they should not be and doing damage. Or they could develop a character fungus that chokes them along the way. Or, as not all plants become trespassers, not all children act out in the "yards" of others. Some just choke and stifle themselves in their own growth. As an unpruned vine can get entwined in its own branches, so can children get so wrapped up in themselves and their own growth that they are unable to handle it. They don't act out, but they "implode." They get depressed, withdraw, are fearful, or suffer from lack of confidence. They may turn to substance abuse or some other way of retreating from life.

Thus, the first reason that quantity of time is important is that since growth is happening anyway—and it happens continuously—you must be there throughout the process. This takes a lot of time. You cannot "skip" time. Even though you are not with children every moment, or even every day at times, you need to be involved in the process throughout. The gardener waters a plant and then leaves it alone to grow, but she is monitoring the plant's progress to see if it looks dehydrated or waterlogged. Children are not a project you can work on for a while and then put away until you have more time. They are growing all the time, so you have to be around to monitor their growth.

The second reason why quantity of time is important is that since children internalize things from the outside world as they grow, you have to be ever-present, monitoring the things they internalize. The analogy here is filling a car's tank with gas. A child's system is taking in things from you along the way as a car takes in gasoline and converts it to energy. A child takes in love and structure and converts them into character. It takes you time to fill the car's tank, and it takes the engine time to use the fuel to produce energy to get to the destination. The engine can't suck down all twenty gallons at once and get you to your destination instantly. It uses a quantity of fuel over time. You cannot feed it all at once. It has to be spread out.

In similar fashion, the quantity of love and discipline you give must be metabolized over time with the child. It must be taken in, understood, turned into neurological structures in the brain, practiced in the body with experience, corrected by that experience, reinternalized in a different fashion, and given more fuel to consolidate it. This linear process takes large quantities of time from the parent. The parent must distribute the fuel as the child needs it. You can't give it all in a "quality" moment, because then the child cannot use it over the process.

The third reason why quantity of time is important is that children need to grow in relationship with another person in order to develop character. One of the biggest problems that some people have is that various aspects of their personalities have been developed outside of relationship. Let me illustrate with an adult example.

Debbie, who was thirty-five, came to me because she was experiencing anxiety. She was a competent person with many gifts; yet, when she needed to stand up for her ideas in certain work situations, she would become very anxious. The mere thought of telling her colleagues what she was thinking scared her into an anxious state. She was afraid to bring certain parts of herself into relationship. When she got close to letting others see who she was, what she was thinking, and what she wanted, she became afraid. The same fear drove her to choose friends who were insensitive and did not want to hear her needs. When people are afraid to bring some aspect of themselves into relationships, they often pick people who are incapable of relating to them the way they need.

When Debbie was growing up, her parents were unavailable when she needed to experience those assertive aspects of herself. One parent was absent, and the other was threatened by her assertiveness. So she kept those aspects of herself hidden, causing anxiety. She was anxious for two reasons: first, those parts of herself were not available to her when she needed them, and second, when she felt them, she would fear punishment. In addition, because she was afraid to stand up for herself, she was vulnerable to people taking advantage of her.

So your child needs to experience all of the aspects of himself with you. He needs to bring the following aspects of himself into relational experience with you over time:

- Needs
- Weakness
- Vulnerability
- Hurt
- Sadness
- Anger
- Strength
- Failure
- Talents
- Opinions
- Assertiveness
- Honesty
- Sexuality

When you spend time with all aspects of your child, he is able to integrate all of those aspects of himself into relationships and not have hidden, split-off parts to his character. But those experiences take quantities of time. In reality, experience equals time. Make sure that you are not just passing time, but relating to all the different aspects of your child in the above list.

Thus, for all of those reasons, quality time is not enough. It takes quantity as well. Spend time with your child, and it will come back to you and many others in hundreds of ways.

The Way the Process Works

Stacy came in for counseling with her son, Scott. She was worried because three-year-old Scott was not learning immediate obedience. When I asked her what she meant by "immediate obedience," she told me that she had learned at her church that children should be obedient the first time they are told something if they are to have good character. I did not ask her if she always "got it right the first time" in life, but I was appalled that she expected that from her son.

Teaching and internalizing character require a certain kind of experience of time, not just "knowledge." Internalizing a new skill, habit, or moral teaching is a process—one that involves ignorance, failure, and disobedience on the part of the child, and discipline, encouragement, and teaching on the part of the parent. The process goes something like this:

1. Introduce children to the reality. Children do not know something before they learn it or are told it. They must be taught or shown a concept, rule, or behavior before they understand it. This may mean that Dad says, "Throw the ball this way," or Mom says, "Pick up the clothes on the floor of your room before dinner." Sometimes parents expect a child to know right from wrong before they learn it!

   The first thing the child may hear is anger about the infraction. "How could you have done this?!" Children who are taught with anger develop anxiety, fear, and uncertainty. I had to teach Stacy that the first time she told Scott something, or corrected him, she did not need to use a disapproving or angry tone of voice. Scott often did not understand what she expected him to do.

2. Allow children to hit the reality limit of their ability. Children will fail when they try something new. If they are learning a new skill, they will not get it right the first time. On their first attempt to get the food into their mouth, they may hit their cheek. Their first shot at the basketball hoop may land on the hood of the car.

   If they are learning a new rule, they may not obey it the first time because of inherent rebellion. In this case, the parent sets the limit by stepping in and saying that to disobey a rule is "not okay," and prescribing some consequence. Failure is part of the process. Children run into the discipline of the parent and find out that reality is bigger than they are.

3. Transform the failure. When a child fails or is disciplined, there is usually an emotional component to that event. The emotional component to a small failure, like falling down, may be too negligible to notice. But some failure and discipline hurt. The child may be sad or angry. In these cases, the parent must empathize with and contain the child's feelings. Empathizing and containing are crucial to the process because they reestablish the parent's emotional connection with the child and win him over eventually to the side of reality and truth.

"I know, honey. It's hard to have to do this. I understand" are some of the empathic statements you can use. Empathy paves the way for the child to identify with the limit or the reality of his performance. In contrast, anger, guilt, and shame distance him from the reality he needs to internalize.

4. Help the child to identify with the reality. If the parent succeeds at transforming the failure—that is, if the child feels understood and loved while he sees the reality of his actions—he is ready to identify with the reality. He will take in the reality of the rule, the concept, or the needed growth step for the skill, and move forward. It becomes part of him. He says, in effect, "Oh, I see."

5. Encourage your child to try again. Learning takes more than one try. In learning new skills, children have to try and fail, and then try again. They have to assimilate the knowledge that they learned in the failure and make adjustments inside of them. Then they try again, and we find out where they are. The process of correction, metabolizing, and internalizing is repeated.

While I had to explain to Stacy that she had a point in wanting her child to learn to obey her when she asked, he was just in the beginning stages of learning. She was going to have to walk him through the process. While we do not advocate allowing disobedience from a child who "knows better," sometimes parents expect children to understand a rule, or the idea of obedience itself, without ever going through the disciplinary process that teaches children the very obedience parents desire.

Character development requires experience. You cannot tell a child how to do something and instantly expect him to do it correctly. You must walk him through the process, help him when he fails, and aid him in making normal failure a learning experience that becomes part of his character.

These learning steps are a specific sequence of events in time. This is why parenting takes time and cannot be done from a distance. The child needs time to go through the experience, and the parent needs time to discipline and to empathize with the child's failure. To illustrate, let's go back to the example of my coach. Kayo Dottley says, "Run the ball in between the guard and the tackle." Then Tommy runs (wrongly) around the end. Kayo steps in and says, "No, not that way! You'll get killed!" (I can still see Kayo's animated gestures as he emphasizes the point.) Tommy feels the impact of the defense hitting him as he tries to go the wrong way with no blocking (hitting the reality). He also feels the correction of the big coach. He takes a moment to metabolize that pain with a little encouragement to get back up. He tries it again. It goes well, and now he "gets it." The next time, Tommy knows what to do and does it, without Kayo's nagging. It has become a part of who he is. The experience has become character.

The Time the Child Needs

Most parents realize that they must spend time with their children, but sometimes spending time is not enough. You also have to know how a child uses time to become a mature person. In fact, the biblical word for "mature" includes time in its definition. Part of the word means to "set out to a particular point or a goal." Another part of the word means to "ripen." Just as we give a plant time to ripen, we need to give a child seasons of experience to mature. Let's look at why time is important for the child.

Time-specific Steps

Recently I was talking to a mother with a fifteen-month-old daughter. She expected her little girl to be talking in sentences! I was astounded as I watched their interaction. The only thing that I could think about was the little girl's confusion as she tried to understand what her mother wanted. The distance between her ability and her mother's expectation was vast.

You cannot accomplish something "before its time." For example, you cannot teach an infant how to read; reading belongs to the school-age years. You cannot teach a preschooler about dating; that belongs to the teen years. You cannot teach certain motor skills before a child is neurologically and physically ready. You must wait until "it is time."

Do not think you are going to have better children if you push them to learn things early! Parents who push their children are more concerned about themselves and their feelings of pride and accomplishment than what is good for the child. Children may not be ready for what you expect of them; you may harm them if you require them to do things for which they are not ready. As the apostle Paul told the Corinthians, "I gave you milk, not solid food, for you were not yet ready for it. Indeed, you are still not ready" (1 Corinthians 3:2).

Broadly speaking, children develop along a predictable path. Let's look at a normal timeline for a child's development.

The first year, a child creates a bond with her parents and learns to trust. She must establish a healthy dependency and learn that being a part of a relationship is a good thing. As an infant learns how to attach securely, she develops physically and cognitively as well. She spends most of the first year having her needs met and finding out that she is wanted. You cannot spoil an infant by loving her too much! Hold her often and comfort her distress. Meet her needs in the early time of life when she is totally dependent and helpless.

Beginning around the second year, discipline and language enter the scene. The child is learning to be a separate person and beginning to get more mobile, eventually walking. She finds out what a limit is. She adds no to her vocabulary, and your task is to learn how to respond to it. You need to be present for your child while she learns independence, and she needs to be able to run back to you for refueling her need for security. Be available to your child, and give her time to test her budding autonomy. When she goes too far, or does something you have taught her not to do, give her a limit. But remember, she is just learning, so give her enough experience to know what she is doing wrong before you discipline her.

Soon thereafter, a child finds out that you are not going to do everything for her, and she has to cope with a few more rules and a few more structures. She begins to learn about morals as well as the difference between her and her brother. Play becomes paramount, her way of "going to the office."

In the childhood years, the group is important. A child needs to learn how to operate in the group. In the school-age years, a child rapidly learns skill development and social behavior. Somewhere else besides home, she learns appropriate behavior and many new skills and activities.

Adolescents almost begin life anew. Independence is at a whole new level. Sexuality is budding. Dating and opposite-sex relationships enter the scene. A child questions her morals, values, and ethics. The peer group becomes a powerful influence, and you need not only to provide guidelines, but also to begin letting go.

The following table illustrates some of the tasks at different stages of development:

STAGE	TASK
Infancy	Trust
	Dependency
	Attachment
	Physiological regulation (sleeping, eating patterns, physical growth)
	Emerging orienting behaviors towards the attachment figure
	Learning to be soothed by external comforting
Later Infancy and Toddlerhood	Increasing physical development with corresponding interaction with the environment
	Increasing mobility beginning with crawling and eventually walking
	Increasing exploration of the world around them as curiosity increases
	Beginning to use and understand language
	Learning to understand and respect limits
	In toddlerhood, learning that open defiance is going to be futile
	Learning increasing independence and separateness
	Introduction to rules
Early Childhood Years	New skills of play, talents and other abilities such as sports, art, and music
	New skills of relationships and social interactions
	Increasing intellectual development

	Learning to obey rules and outside authorities
	Moral and spiritual development
	Respecting other people and property
	Beginning sex education
Adolescence	New physical changes to be integrated as adult physiology becomes a reality
	The emergence of sexuality
	Expanding moral development to include sexuality
	Expanding moral development to include principles and principle thinking as well as rules
	Changing the relationship with parents to reflect greater maturity
	Increasing independence
	Increasing skills of interacting with the opposite sex and dating
	Further development of talents and strengths discovered in pre-teen years
	Getting more focused about personal interests and strengths
	Questioning and discovering values
	Seeking deeper spiritual understanding
	Finding and fitting into peer group
	Discovering and dealing with reality of peer pressure
	Preparing for leaving home

One reason why parents should not expect too much too young is that there are critical windows of time for certain developmental tasks. The general thinking is that children need to go through these stages at the appropriate time because windows open up at a certain time in a child's development. For example, certain areas of the brain develop at certain ages, and a child needs to have age-appropriate experiences to match those changes in the brain.

If holding and bonding are missed, or rushed, for example, it is more difficult for a child to "make it up later." Or, if discipline comes too late, then powerful rage develops out of control and becomes an enduring personality trait. That is why it is so important to let your child be who she needs to be at that time, not forcing her to be older than she is. She has certain appropriate tasks for each age. As Solomon said, "There is a time for everything, and a season for every activity under heaven" (Ecclesiastes 3:1).

Let your children have the full timeline God designed for them. When the recipe for a cake says, "Bake at 350 degrees for 1 hour," the cake needs a full hour. A child needs to have the necessary time it takes to go through her stages. If we are impatient, we try to harvest "maturity" before our child is ripe. Some apples are sour, not because they are spoiled, but because they have been rushed. Don't rush your child; enjoy the process of growing up and maturing. As many parents have said, "They change too fast!" One day, before you know it, your children will be grown up. Enjoy them while they are getting there.

Remember All Three

We have talked about the time you must put in, the way this time gets structured, and the time a child needs. We feel strongly about time as an ingredient necessary for growth. But let us remind you of one of our favorite terms: integration. Integrate the ingredient of time with the other two ingredients of grace and truth. In our workshops for parents we always give a formula that goes like this:

Grace + Truth over Time = Growth

You need all three ingredients to bring about growth. Giving grace and truth for a weekend, or once a month, is not going to do it. That is a "retreat" mentality. Giving only truth over time will fail also. That is a prison. And, in like fashion, giving only grace over time is disastrous. That equals bedlam! A child needs to know that you are on his side, and that is grace. He needs to know that you will give him reality, and that is truth. And he needs it pretty much every day, from birth to his late teens. Take a deep breath, and have a good time!

Now that you know the three ingredients you need to raise a great kid, in the next section of the book we will describe how you can go about using them in developing the six character traits every child needs to become a mature adult.

Part Two

Developing the Six Character Traits Every Child Needs

—— Four ——

Laying the Foundation of Life

Connectedness

Chris's parents called him their "low-maintenance child." He had three siblings, and Mom and Dad were stressed and preoccupied not only with the other kids but also with their demanding work and financial situation. His folks admitted he didn't get a lot of attention as a baby, but at the same time, he hadn't seemed to need much.

While his brothers had behavioral and academic problems that demanded much parental time, Chris seemed to do well without parental intervention, even preferring to be on his own. He was quiet, bright, responsible, and self-sufficient. Early on, Chris learned to tie his shoes, clean his room, and organize his homework.

When I (Dr. Townsend) visited Chris's family during his grade-school years, I would interact with the kids as best a boring grown-up can. They were all engaging and relational—except Chris. Although he was polite and would talk about his life and activities, he seemed aloof and "not there." He wasn't angry, or self-centered. What I experienced was more of an absence of his emotional self than the presence of anything bad.

About this time, Chris's teachers started sending in reports of social problems at school. They noted social withdrawal, lack of friendships, and avoidance. Concerned, his parents tried to get him more connected to friends. They arranged parties, times with friends, and other activities. They made sure to ask him about his day when he returned from school.

But it was as though they were asking Chris to speak another language. He liked being busy, and he liked people at a distance.

He simply did not desire close relationships. When his dad would sit down with him to get him to "open up," Chris had no feelings to report, no struggles to discuss, and no need to talk about himself.

Dad would ask, "So how's school?"

"Fine," Chris would reply in a friendly but closed manner.

"Who do you play with?"

"Oh, different people."

"Any problems with them or with your schoolwork?"

"No, everything's fine."

Chris would answer his dad's questions, but he would shift uncomfortably in his chair until the "time" was over. Then, relieved, he would go shoot hoops or read a book, back in his own element. Chris was comfortable in his own world, which had many good things in it, but no people. And he wasn't lonely. He was simply not able to experience a need for relationships.

Life Equals Relationship

Chris's problem is perhaps the most foundational one in growing up. Because he was unable to make attachments, he was separated from life itself. He didn't experience a need for connection, but he was suffering from this lack of it.

Attachment is the capacity to relate to God and others, to connect to something outside of ourselves. When we make an attachment, good things are transferred between us and others, such as empathy, comfort, truth, and encouragement. Attachment brings warmth, meaning, and purpose to life. Of all the character aspects we will deal with in this book, this is the most important. As the Bible teaches, love (which is closely related to attachment) never fails (1 Corinthians 13:8). When we connect deeply and lovingly with God and significant people, we can weather many of the storms of life.

From the womb, your child is designed to connect. When she leaves the womb, she is in a state of isolation, terror, and anger. She is utterly alone in her experience, with no good things within or without her. Birth is a jarring experience for infants.

The instinctual, God-given response of a baby's mother is to bring the baby to herself, to soothe and calm her, and to begin the process of attachment that helps the baby experience the good that exists in relationship.

Relationship brings us out of our natural tendency to be disconnected and self-sufficient. We are by nature isolated, distrustful, and afraid to reach out. When we are disconnected, we create our own distorted realities and opinions about life and ourselves. There is no source of reality that grounds us into the truth.

Some may quarrel with the idea that the ability to attach is a character trait. Attachment doesn't seem to resonate with things like morality, integrity, and right thinking. It is, however, very much a part of the basic functions of a person. When a person is loved and treated well, she attaches to the person who loves her and treats her well. She gains a sense that being loved and treated well is a good thing. In addition, she learns how to love and treat others well. This is the basis of the Golden Rule, the foundation of all morality (Matthew 7:12). An attached person has the structures within herself to become a moral person.

Attachment is not humanity's idea, but God's. God himself is relational at his core: He is love (1 John 4:8). In some fashion that we don't understand, the Father, Son, and Spirit are attached and related to each other at all times. God may experience isolation from us when we distance from him, but the persons of the Trinity are always in relationship with one another.

The Importance of Attachment

We cannot overemphasize the importance of developing your child's ability to attach. All of the tasks of life are based, at some level, on how attached we are to God and others. Kids who are emotionally connected in healthy ways are more secure. They delay gratification. They respond to discipline. They deal with failure. They make good moral decisions. The list goes on and on. You cannot lose by developing your child's ability to relate.

The reason is simple: *the attached child is never left without a way to get the resources for life.* Life brings many demands, problems, and requirements. The connected child looks within himself for what he can provide, then goes to God and others for the rest. The detached child is left to fend for himself, and he does not have sufficient resources to conduct life on his own.

My friend Betty was recently describing the differences between her two sons. Seven-year-old Dylan was an "outie." You always knew where he was emotionally. Good, bad, or green, he was clear as to how he felt about life. Ten-year-old Spencer was an "innie." No amount of coaxing would get him out of his shell.

Betty had been struck by this difference when both had encountered problems at school. Both of the boys were somewhat overweight. Some kids called Dylan "Fatty." Normally a happy kid, he had burst into tears after walking in the door, and he sobbed while his mom held him. Then, after they talked about the situation, Dylan and his mom came up with some plans to solve the problem. His folks got him on a good diet and weight program. They coached him on how to handle his friends. They alerted the school about the situation, for those instances in which things might get too brutal. Within a few weeks, Dylan's situation was much better.

Dylan knew he couldn't deal with the problem by himself. At the end of his rope, he went to his parents and received comfort, support, and structure so that together they could solve the problem. This is how we are to operate throughout life.

When Spencer was teased about his weight, no one knew for weeks. He began to withdraw more into himself. He began to behave aggressively. He started arguing with teachers and fighting with other kids. He became withdrawn and spent long periods of time in his room. His grades took a dive. It took a great deal of time and effort to find that he was being teased by other children, and his lack of connection cost him a lot. Spencer's problem was not that he didn't have enough resources to solve the problem. This is the human condition. His problem was that he wasn't able to reach out to family and friends to meet life's demands.

Infancy: The Birthplace of Attachment (0–12 months)

Research supports the biblical idea that relationship is crucial to life. Interactions between mother and child deeply affect an infant's developing neurological structures. The literal hardwiring of an infant's brain, including such basic functions as thinking, relating to the world, perceiving, and judging, depends on the mother-child relationship. Severe disruption of this attachment in the early months after birth can affect a child's entire life.

Much evidence points to the fact that an infant's very survival depends on relationship. In some extremely severe cases, otherwise physically healthy infants have actually died without the soothing and love of mother figures to sustain them.

The early attachment between mother and child has deep spiritual implications. God brings a child to trust in him while at his mother's breast (Psalm 22:9). The very act of learning to take in the goodness and nurture of the breast prepares your baby for taking in God's love and care. The mother's nursing readies a child for an eternal and transcendent attachment. What a picture of learning trust and love!

Many people become concerned that children who attach and are dependent will become insecure adults who can't stand on their own. Actually, the opposite is true. The child who is allowed to emotionally depend on a reliable, loving parent becomes fortified with the assurance of her stability. As a child internalizes her mother's love, she feels safe enough to explore the world confidently.

The first year of life is therefore critical to the development of attachment capacities in a child. Although you will always be involved in helping her relate to the outside world, the most fundamental changes come during the first twelve months.

Attachment Goals for Your Child

The ability to connect can be broken down into different categories. Again, while the foundational "inviting to life" work is done in the first year, helping your child with bonding experiences continues through his childhood.

Use Relationship for Equilibrium

Good attachment stabilizes children. Many people can attest to being greatly upset at some problem or loss, and when they were connected to a loving, structured person, they felt calmer and were able to think more clearly and productively about their situation. This aspect emerges during the first few weeks of life as the infant uses his mother's presence and orderliness to achieve what is called *homeostasis*. This physiological and emotional regulatory process also involves stability in things like sleep, feeding, and schedule.

Parents can help children have equilibrium at all ages by providing not just bonding and love, but by being engaged, safe, and predictable. God quiets his people with his love (Zephaniah 3:17), so you can quiet your child's turmoil with your attachment.

Learn Basic Trust and Need

Your child needs to learn that being in relationship is the best way to live. During the first few months of life, she is not very aware of mother as a separate person. However, she is aware of warmth and goodness, and she begins to trust that this warmth and goodness will always be there when she needs it.

Basic trust is your child's ability to see the world of relationships as having enough goodness for her. She learns that reaching out to connect is worth doing and that it is reasonably safe enough to do. Children who have established basic trust tend to be hopeful people; they expect that if they reach the end of themselves, good relationships will sustain them.

You can help foster basic trust by being a "good-enough" parent—that is, being responsive at the right times and in the right ways without being perfect, being just a lot more good than bad.

You can help your children develop basic trust during the later years of childhood by drawing out their insecurities and fears of closeness, addressing them, rewarding them for taking risks, and challenging them to trust themselves and other "safe" people. For example, a dad may see that his teen is distressed but silent. The teen may fear that if he opens up and depends on his dad, he will regress to a needy state and lose all the freedom he cherishes. The dad can invite the teen to talk and promise that unless there's some major rule being broken, he just wants to be there and to understand. This can help the teen learn that trust is a good experience.

Value Relationships

Kids need to see not only that connection is good, but also that having specific people in their lives is positive, too. This begins in the first year of life, but continues on. One aspect of maturity is our being able to value and appreciate others' love and sacrifice for us. For children, this creates important traits like a grateful heart for others and the ability to seek out and connect to people who treat us right. When children aren't taught to value people, as adults they may use them only for their own comfort and then discard them. These people casually get out of relationships when they become inconvenient and cause great pain and hurt all around them. They have learned that relationship only exists for them, that the other person has no feelings or rights. Or they may pick people indiscriminately, without regard to the person's character. When they grow up, they sometimes have problems picking safe people. Their lack of understanding may cause them to invest in people who are irresponsible, charming, deceptive, or controlling.

Children need to learn to discern character in others. But sometimes a parent has a hard time explaining character discernment, as they too have the same difficulty. A good resource is our book *Safe People*, which shows how to pick good people and avoid bad ones.

Help your child become a people-oriented person. Talk to her and listen to her. Assist her in talking about how you and she feel about each other. Show gratitude for the good things she does. Require gratitude from her. Let your child know how her actions affect you. If her attitude hurts your feelings or angers you, tell her. Don't ask her to parent you or fix you, but let her know that you will not allow yourself to be treated in disrespectful or harmful ways. Help her to see that while she is loved and unique, she has no special privileges in the family, and she is a team member like anyone else.

Internalize Love

An important milestone for your child is to be able to soothe himself when you are not there. To achieve this independence, you need to shift from an external presence in his life to an internal one. Your child's many experiences of safety and consistency combine over time into a stable, internal mental and emotional representation of you. In times of aloneness, stress, loss, or conflict, your child can draw upon this picture and feel soothed, stable, loved, and structured. He can then use this picture to solve problems or make decisions.

The task of having an internal parent is completed ideally at about three years, but matures all through life. Ultimately, a child no longer experiences this parent inside him, but as part of his very self. He doesn't think, "Mom loves me, so I'm okay," but, "I'm a loved person, and I'm okay."

You can help your child with this important task. Be there in quantity, not just quality. There is no substitute for the many, many loving experiences with you that your child needs to internalize. Provide many occasions when you are there for his needs. As he matures, however, gradually induce him to draw upon the internal love rather than you all the time. This helps him become more independent. Going to sleep in his own bed, learning to feed himself, and allowing baby-sitters to take care of him are all part of this process.

Develop Capacity for Loss

An important task through all of childhood is developing the capacity to experience loss. When we lose someone or something we love, we are faced with the reality of living in a fallen world, one that most of us aren't really prepared for. But success in life involves learning to deal with loss.

Attached children learn to protest, mourn, and resolve their losses. Children need to attach to people and things so, when they lose something, they can bring their sad feelings to these people, who will help them let go of what they have lost. When children don't attach, several bad things can happen. They may devalue what they lost: "I didn't want that doll anyway." They may stay stuck in a protest mode: "But I want it!" They may chronically mourn: "I don't care how long it's been, I still miss my doll." All these are hurtful to your child and can cause problems in adulthood.

A capacity for loss helps children accept the world as it is. It also helps them love and value people they miss and look for others like those they have lost. Crying and sadness are a part of this process and a mark of maturity. Sympathize with your child's loss. Say, "You're right, it's really sad that we couldn't go to your favorite restaurant tonight. I know you wanted to go pretty badly." But keep appropriate limits so that your child doesn't become sad so that you will feel sorry for him and let him have what he wants.

Help your child value good things. But also help her protest, let go, and resolve losses. The capacity to mourn a loss and to move on after mourning is a mark of maturity: wise people are in the house of mourning (Ecclesiastes 7:4).

Develop Gender Roles

As kids grow into the preschool years, they begin learning how to attach to people of the same sex and of the opposite sex in distinctive ways. Little boys want both to be like and to compete with Dad; little girls do the same with Mom. Girls want to marry their dad, and boys, their mom. Parents need to contain and structure these intense feelings for their kids. Mom needs to reassure her son of her love for him, but at the same time tell him, "I'm married to Dad, so I'm taken. But you will later be able to find someone special for yourself." And Dad needs to accept and deal with his son's competitive attitudes toward him. At the same time, he needs to insist on the fact that he is still the boss, and these things will have to be worked out with that reality in place.

Relate to the World

Children use relationship as a springboard of safety from which to explore the world of preschool, games, imagination, sports, and peers. They are very busy getting invested in the universe, and they need to draw from their relationship to their parents. Parents need to listen to and help make sense of the many interests the child has. Attachment helps children sort through what they like and don't like.

For example, a child will chatter to his mom about his plans to be a firefighter. She listens, draws him out, and helps him develop his interest in the outside world.

Develop Give and Take

Another aspect of growing up is learning that relationships require give and take. This ability develops during the early school years. The other person doesn't exist for the child and also has needs that have to be met in this relationship. Relationships cost something. If both parties do their part in carrying the yoke of responsibility for the relationship, things go well and both people grow. If the child still sees the connection only in terms of her interests, she will have great conflict with people later in life. Either good people won't put up with her, or sick people will let her use them and neither will grow.

Reward your child for, and set limits on, her involvement in the day, welfare, and feelings of other family members as a basic attachment responsibility. You might say, "When you're done talking about your school day, ask the person next to you about their day." Don't reward bad and selfish attitudes. When she doesn't show interest in others, let her suffer consequences for that. Mutual love requires practice and experience.

Teach Altruism

The most mature attachment skill is selfless giving. Altruism is giving out of concern for another without regard to oneself. It is the essence of God's love. God sent his Son to die for us while we were still sinners (Romans 5:8). Altruism has no other agenda, no other motive, except the welfare of the other.

In one sense, the phrase "altruistic child" is an oxymoron, as growing up is a pretty self-centered endeavor. A childish person is often a self-oriented person; the two traits go together. But in another sense, kids can learn all the way through life that they can comfort with the comfort that they themselves have received (2 Corinthians 1:3–4).

As you show selfless love (not martyr love, but a love based on free and good-natured choice) to your child, you give her the fuel to give that back at some point. Show not only empathy, but also gratitude to her when she does a favor for you. Reward her when she shows compassion for her friends. Let her see your altruism toward other people and encourage the same in her. You are building on her attachment capacities so that she can be a truly loving person, the highest goal.

How Attachment Happens

Specific tasks create the ability to connect. The child has his job, and the mother (or the primary caregiver) has hers. These two jobs interact to help the child become capable of making attachments to people.

The child must experience the reality that relationship is good and that it brings the necessary elements of life. When your child learns this emotionally, he structures his existence to seek relationship to sustain him. He becomes relationally-oriented rather than self-oriented.

The mother's task is to invite her child from isolation into relationship. This invitation, or wooing of sorts, takes many experiences in order to bear fruit. The mother behaves and responds to the child in a fashion tailored to his particular situation and need. For example, she pays close attention to her child's differing cries, so as to meet his appropriate need for comfort, warmth, changing, or safety. He learns during these times that reaching outside himself for help brings things he needs.

All this is designed to help the child not only take in love, but also perceive love as a good thing, as something to go after in life. Below is a breakdown of the tasks involved on both the child's and the mother's sides.

The Child's Tasks

Experience, and Respond to, the Need for Relationship

Needs drive us to risk attachment. From birth on, as a trigger for action, your child is designed to experience the discomfort of what are called "need states." When he is lonely, afraid, anxious, hurt, or hungry, he needs to pay attention to this discomfort and respond to it in some way. He may cry, fuss, call out for help, or come home from school in tears, as Dylan did. The child learns to take initiative by protesting, reaching out, and getting the parent's attention.

Don't underestimate the value of crying and fussing. These are the primary signals a child has to communicate his discomfort to the world. The very sounds that irritate you are a survival mechanism designed by God. In fact, many believe crying is designed to be irritating to get your attention!

Children grow in attachment by experiencing both relational and functional needs. Relational needs are those that are met simply through the connection itself (comfort, encouragement, love, and affection). Functional needs may involve relationship, but are primarily met through "doing" (changing a diaper, feeding, playing baseball, helping with homework). Functional need experiences help the child learn that reaching out brings good. Relational need experiences, however, are more valuable than functional ones in teaching connectedness to your child. Relationship is always more important than function.

Keep Signaling the Need

Love and support don't always come instantly. Parents aren't available every second, and they may not always know what a child needs. The child's task is to protest long enough for help to get to him. Infants have very little capacity to tolerate being in need for long periods of time, and they shouldn't have to. They are very invested in learning to take in the love they need, and they don't have the ability to wait before going into despair of being rescued. As they get older, and if parents have been consistently there for them, children learn to keep calling or signaling, and help will come.

Receive the Good

A child has many empty places inside him. The younger he is, the emptier he is. One of his main jobs in the first year is to take in love through thousands of loving experiences. As his mother picks him up, coos to him, cuddles him, holds him, and feeds him, he literally internalizes the love he needs to stay alive. The older the child, the less he needs from Mom and Dad, as his earlier experiences become an internal source of comfort and nourishment. Love, however, is something we all need for all of our lives.

A child doesn't receive the good passively. Rather, he goes out to find it and then actively responds to love. He experiences love, takes it in, feels more loved and safe, feels grateful for it, gives the gratitude back, and uses the love to grow and do his tasks in life. Some have a passive idea of bonding, but nothing is more active and requires more initiative and activity than bonding. It's a lot of work.

The Parent's Tasks

Respond to the Need

As caregivers and the source of meeting most of their child's needs, parents must actively be there for attachment needs. Parents need to be attuned and aware of the child's emotional need states. Especially in infancy, the child has no confidence that anyone will be there to help his distress. Discomfort and pain drive him to scream. The parent uses these protests as a call to action in connecting the child to life and showing him that there is someone outside of him who will comfort and sustain him.

Thus, you need to understand the basically empty, loveless, and impotent situation of your child and devote enough time and energy to fill the child up with yourself. You need to be there to pick up, hold, soothe, and feed when the baby signals a need to you. Mainly a child's mother fills these needs in the first year of life.

When mothers are cold and aloof, children often respond with coldness themselves. First they protest, then they go into what is called despair, then into detachment. At this point, to the untrained eye, children may not seem to be any trouble. They are quieter and less fussy. But they are actually in trouble, as they have become cold to the love they need. They have disconnected from life itself. A warm, affectionate mother can prevent this.

Responding to children's needs is a full-time job during the early stages. A mother may need to give up many, many good things to invest time and energy in her child. It is exhausting and taxing work as she gives all she has to someone who has nothing. A mother needs to remember to stay connected to loving, warm, supportive adults during this time, as she can become drained and then be without emotional resources for herself and her baby.

Another aspect of responding to a child's need is *predictability*. Children are not stable inside. Their emotions aren't yet regulated, and they have no sense of security and safety. They are in a constant state of turmoil inside. The consistent "being there" of the parent provides a structure that begins to calm and soothe the child. He is able to take in this structure and rest in it, learning that attachment has an order to it.

Inconsistency here often results in anxious or ambivalent behavior in the child. The child of an inconsistent mother will often be clingy when mother is leaving the room, but then arch away when she returns. The child is stuck in the dilemma of needing someone who is unreliable; he doesn't trust that she won't go away when she finally does arrive to meet his need.

In the first few months of life, some parents interpret an infant's needs as attempts to control and dominate the family. They think that crying and fussing show a child's sinful nature and point toward selfishness. These parents become concerned about giving in to these "destructive demands" of their kids. They will, for example, feed the baby based on a schedule rather than his cries. By doing this, they hope to instill in the infant the reality that he can't play God and that if he gives up control and submits to the parent's timetable, he will be okay.

It is certainly true that we are all born selfish sinners (Romans 3:23). And it is also true that a major task of parents is to help their children give up self-serving attitudes and learn to submit to reality and serve others. However, to interpret an infant's cries as an attempt to dominate is missing the mark for a couple of reasons.

First, not all requests and protests are selfish. God teaches us to ask for what we need and to ask aggressively, like the widow who knocked on the door of the judge (Luke 18:1–8). We have self-centeredness, and we have God-given needs. They are two separate things.

Second, an infant's job is to learn to exist in the world, to need, to trust, and to relate to his mother. His overwhelming emptiness and helplessness don't leave him much room to want to be the next Hitler. He is more concerned with making it minute-by-minute in a strange, scary environment. The parent who ascribes sinful motives to an infant can do serious damage to his sense of self, his ability to trust, and his capacity to protest and later take responsibility for himself. This damage can even extend to physical health. A condition known as "failure to thrive," meaning that the infant's physical growth becomes retarded, can be related to a parent's denying the appropriate needs of her infant.

We are not saying that a mother should be there every second for her infant and not let him cry. A little crying helps a child own the experience of being responsible for signaling the world that he needs something. It may be good to let him have some discomfort instead of immediately picking him up and inhibiting his developing sense of responsibility

After the first twelve months, the infant has, we hope, taken in many, many safe, predictable, and comforting experiences in response to his demands. Comforting a child creates in him a sense that the world is a reasonably safe place, and he can move on to his next task, exploring that world. Then you can work on helping your child with delay of gratification, patience, learning to self-soothe when you are absent, and some discipline. At this point you can introduce structure and requirements to the child's reality.

Respond Appropriately

The younger the child, the less she is able to tell you the nature of her need. Your task, especially in her infancy, is to figure out what your child needs and respond to it. A need to be burped is different from a need to be comforted out of loneliness. Babies have very little tolerance for the time it takes to figure this out; you have to be tolerant for both of you. Many are the parents who have tried holding, feeding, walking, changing, and even sitting on an operating clothes dryer with a squalling infant who is letting them know, "I'm still miserable!"

Later in life, you should require your child to own her need and to ask for help. For example, if an eleven-year-old says, "I miss my friend," she is stating a need, but not asking for help. If you immediately call a friend and ask her to come over, your daughter learns that she doesn't have to experience the humility and risk of asking for help. Better to ask, "Why don't you think about this, and tell me what you need?" Your daughter may come up with what she really needs—for example, "Time with Mom today."

Present Relational Solutions to Relational Needs

Your child needs connection for her isolation, hurt, loneliness, and so forth. She needs answers, suggestions, advice, and problem solving for her functional needs. She does not have the ability to distinguish one from the other. Your task is to ensure that your child learns that relationship comes before anything. Help her connect by being understanding, being warm, listening well, and being empathic.

Empathy, a critical ability for character development, is feeling the pain or distress of another—an experience that drives one toward another to provide comfort. Empathy is more than an intellectual validation of someone's problem; it originates deep within our soul. Jesus himself allowed empathy to drive him: he "had compassion" for the distress of people (Matthew 9:36). Empathy translates to a child as "you are not alone, you are loved and understood," whether this is performed by cuddling a colicky infant or by saying to a distraught teen, "That is so sad that you and Billy broke up; it must hurt."

There is a psychological term for the mother's task of calmly receiving and containing the anxieties and discomfort of the infant so that the infant can tolerate and slowly accept them for himself over time. That word is *reverie*. Mothers will often experience reverie as almost a dream state, as being lost in the depth of the connection as she holds and rocks the child. She drops her own individuality temporarily to contain the child's experiences.

Simply connecting can solve what sometimes appears to be a functional problem. For instance, when a child whines that he wants to go outside with his friends during homework time, sometimes simply saying, "I know it's tough to miss your buddies" will result in the child's quieting down and finishing his homework. Love covers a multitude of sins (1 Peter 4:8).

Similarly, be aware of the tendency to solve relational problems functionally. The exhausted mother sticks a bottle in the needy infant's mouth. A dad gives a lonely child a toy with which to amuse himself. A mom gives three steps to solving a relationship problem when the child wants her to just listen. Sometimes the child is saying in his own way, "I want you!" Remember how you feel when you want to be understood and a well-meaning friend gives advice instead.

Connect Without Intrusiveness

Make attachment inviting by giving your child a certain amount of freedom and emotional space. Children's bonding needs are not constant. Most needs occur in cycles. When you have met the need for comfort and connection, the intense closeness abates, and your child can be free to digest what he was given. Often, for example, after being comforted, a young child will straight-arm her mother and try to wriggle away. The child uses the fuel of love to begin safely exploring her world. If the parent is nonintrusive, the child feels free to move back toward relationship again, without fear of being smothered.

You need to be aware of this and not intrude on your child's experience. Sometimes an anxious mom will clasp her child too tightly or too long. Sometimes a dad will want to continue a "dad talk" with a child who is done talking and wants to go skateboarding. *Children with intrusive parents experience relationship as controlling or enmeshing.* This is extremely unfortunate, because they then assign bad things to closeness—for example, that it destroys freedom. Children's ability to learn autonomy and initiative can be compromised. They will sometimes react by shutting down emotionally and withdrawing inside to get away from the relationship. Or they will angrily distance, as a teen might to a parent who is holding on too tightly. Many children with intrusive parents struggle greatly with intimacy as adults. They experience closeness as something that will destroy, violate, or imprison them, and they are not able to accept the attachment offered them.

This corresponds with what the Bible teaches about the nature of love: it is not self-seeking (1 Corinthians 13:5). Love desires the freedom of the other; it does not seek to comfort itself, but the other; it only requires that it be received as needed. The good parent invites but does not demand connection the child doesn't need.

This is difficult for many parents. The nature of parenting is to connect, and closeness is the highest value. A parent who has deficits in attachment himself may be trying to get his dependency needs met through his child. Although you might think, "The more closeness, the better for my child," if you demand closeness to meet your own needs, if it inhibits freedom and mastery, or if it robs the child of experience, love can become something your child dreads instead of seeks.

Parent your child to be able safely to receive and give love and connectedness. You are helping build a connected foundation inside her that will sustain her for life. This is also the necessary building block for the aspect of character we will be discussing in the next chapter: learning responsibility.

Five

Developing Self-Control

Responsibility

Recently I (Dr. Townsend) attended a neighborhood picnic with my wife and kids. It was fun walking around, visiting with other families, and catching up. We stopped to chat with Sharon and Ted, a couple with whom we are friends. As we were talking, Anthony, their eight-year-old son ran up, out of breath, and held out a melting Popsicle to Sharon. "Mom, they're having a sack race and I need to be in it and I can't find a trash can and they're almost starting and please, Mom, please, please, please!"

Sharon instinctively reached out and took the glob from Anthony, who smiled his thanks and rushed off to join the all-important race. It happened so fast that we all just stood there a moment looking at each other. Then we all burst out laughing at the situation. When we had quieted down, Sharon said, "Meet childhood: they make the mess, and we get sticky."

Sharon's observation on Anthony and his Popsicle is a metaphor for childhood. Kids hand their problems, mistakes, and crises to their parents. Left to their own devices, their approach is, "My life is my parents' problem. They'll take care of things for me. My job is simply to make sure I get them to clean up my messes in life." This philosophy extends from attitudes to academics to moral issues.

The task of parenting is to transform the child's stance from "My life is my parents' problem" to "Yikes, my life is *my* problem. A melting Popsicle and a sack race deadline cause a problem I shouldn't look to someone else to solve. Though my parents love me, they aren't going to clean up all the messes I make in life."

And this is the second great aspect of character building: the capacity to take responsibility for one's life.

Responsibility Puts Love into Action

Every caring parent wants her child to do well in life. "Doing well" has to do with the functional aspects of living, how one performs. This might mean many things, such as having a good job, being successful financially, or simply being an honest, hardworking person.

The key to all these wishes of a parent is responsibility. The child who learns that responsibility is his friend is the child who has a head start in life. We define responsibility as *the capacity to own one's life as one's problem.* No matter what my problem, situation, or circumstances, the buck stops with me. Responsible people are much more apt to be successful in their relationships, work, and mission in life. They aren't waiting for someone else to make them successful. They take action and find solutions to their own problems. There is no meeting being conducted somewhere whose agenda is how to make your life better!

Responsible kids have learned that their life is their problem. Even though they are loved, valued, and cherished, they have their own jobs in life. These jobs range anywhere from not running in the house to achieving a certain grade point average. Children are always "working" at something. It is the parent's job to help structure their time and energy into activities that develop responsibility.

Kids who have internalized a sense of responsibility are also free to make good moral decisions. Responsibility leads to freedom. When children "own" their lives, they understand that being responsible makes life run better and that being irresponsible brings bad results. They develop the freedom to behave according to their values instead of reacting to their whims and immaturity. When they face the temptation to have sex outside of marriage, to smoke marijuana, or to hang with the wrong crowd, they have been making free choices in other areas for some time already. They are not imprisoned by their impulses or resentment of authority. They evaluate the situation, and they take the long view of the cost of a bad choice. Because they have earned freedom, they are free to say no to bad things.

The idea of earning freedom to make good moral choices is an important point, because some current teachings say that all you have to do is tell kids to choose good things and refuse bad things, or simply inform them of the dangers of the bad. The first view is a "choice is the answer" solution; the second is the "information is the answer" solution. Choices and information are indeed important, but a child needs to practice self-control, delay of gratification, and setting and receiving limits before he can choose the good and refuse the bad. You may as well think that all a five-year-old needs to stop hitting his three-year-old sister is to say, "Choose to stop, Billy. You need to know that it's bad for her." Billy probably already knows it's bad for her— that's why he's doing it. Other interventions need to occur also.

The primary function of responsibility is to put love into action. We are called to create and develop good relationships in our spheres of influence. God designed us to replicate and expand his nature, both in ourselves and with others. We are here to bring the love he offers to the world. We protect, share, and grow this love by responsibility. It is a sense of responsibility that calls us to do more than experience and enjoy love; we are to develop it. We were created to develop love by performing good works that God foreordained for us (Ephesians 2:10). *Relationship is the reason for existence. Responsibility is the means to bring about and protect relationship.*

Love is never enough. It has always required responsibility to keep it alive. How many marriages do you know that have ended because, though the parties loved one another, someone broke their covenant to be responsible to love, cherish, and not violate their duties to the other? A wife I knew had a husband who was continually deceptive. He lied about their finances, his habits, and his work. She tried and tried to regain some sense of closeness with him after each revelation. But finally, she told me, "I don't feel the love anymore, because I can't trust him." Mutual trust, respect, honor, and integrity keep love nourished. Love withers and dies when someone transgresses the line of responsibility too often.

From the beginning, life included love and work. Adam and Eve were in a state of unbroken attachment, both with God and with each other. Yet they weren't simply to sit around and "be" in a state of bliss. They had demanding jobs: "God blessed them and said to them, 'Be fruitful and increase in number; fill the earth and subdue it. Rule over the fish of the sea and the birds of the air and over every living creature that moves on the ground'" (Genesis 1:28). They were responsible for certain tasks, even in a perfect universe.

Responsible people have developed many abilities, beginning in childhood, that bode them well in the challenges and opportunities of life:

- Making decisions
- Solving problems
- Being truthful even when it hurts
- Structuring love
- Taking initiative
- Having self-control
- Resisting evil
- Saying no to what is not right for them
- Being free to choose
- Owning one's mistakes and learning from them
- Performing good deeds
- Being an actively involved person
- Delaying gratification
- Persevering
- Living according to one's values
- Entering into conflict for justice and righteousness
- Having integrity and virtues
- Protecting the weak and oppressed

Attachment and responsibility were designed to grow together in your child, in the same way that love and truth are to be integrated in your parenting. When these don't go together, the child and his world both suffer. For example, many very attached, irresponsible children are loving, connecting, and engaging, but they can be unreliable at best and totally out of control at worst. Have you ever seen the "cute" child who, though he feels quite loved and secure, drives people crazy? He may constantly interrupt the conversation of a group of adults by demanding that they watch him do somersaults. All the while, his parents are beaming at his antics. The child's problem has become everyone else's problem. He is not in control of his life.

When that happens, someone else is paying for the child's lack of control or ownership. A friend of mine swore he would never have kids because of what he saw in the lives of his own friends who did have kids. He had visited a friend who had three teenagers. When he knocked on the door, the teenagers were watching TV in the den. They yelled for Mom to get the door. When he visited, they smiled and were pleasant, but Mom had to ask them to turn the TV down. And he visited his friend in her kitchen, where she was washing the dishes of a meal she had prepared and her children had eaten. When he left, they hadn't shifted from the den.

"If that's what it takes," he told me, "I'm not doing that duty." He saw the kids incurring a debt and their mother paying it for them. Nice kids can be irresponsible kids. Love and limits must go together.

Develop Responsibility With or Without Your Child's Permission

Having a child who takes responsibility for her life is a good and appropriate dream of a parent. Yet there is one fundamental problem: *from the beginning, the child has no interest whatsoever in becoming responsible.* Your child may eagerly bond with you and depend on you, but in taking up her cross of life's burdens (Luke 9:23), your kid will be your adversary—at least in the early stages.

Children can't see value in taking responsibility for a problem. They are, by definition, without self-control. Instead, they are into other-control, mostly by manipulating their parents into taking care of things for them. And, thinking they are loving them, parents often take on responsibilities for their children that the kids should be bearing themselves. Taking such responsibility for your children negates and stifles their ability to shoulder life as they grow up.

Boundaries: Bringing Responsibility to Your Child's Experience

Setting boundaries is a central part of developing responsible character in your child. Boundaries are a person's property line. Invisible, but still very real, they point out where you end and others begin. They allow you to know what belongs to you and what belongs to another. They allow you to know what you are and are not responsible for. Boundaries help you stop bad things from happening to you. For example, when you say no to a controlling person, you are setting a boundary.

God is the originator of boundaries. He draws lines in his own character: the Father, Son, and Holy Spirit are all connected but separate. He defines himself as distinct from his creation: "As the heavens are higher than the earth, so are my ways higher than your ways and my thoughts than your thoughts" (Isaiah 55:9). He is clear about what he loves and what he hates: "For I, the LORD, love justice; I hate robbery and iniquity" (Isaiah 61:8).

As God's image-bearers, we are also to have boundaries. We need to be clear about what we are responsible for: "for each one should carry his own load" (Galatians 6:5). We need to be truthful and honest about what is right and wrong: "speaking the truth in love" (Ephesians 4:15). We need to refuse what God is against: "The deeds of faithless men I hate; they will not cling to me" (Psalm 101:3).

Our book *Boundaries: When to Say Yes, When to Say No to Take Control of Your Life* (Zondervan, 1992) deals with setting limits to develop freedom and self-control and with resisting controlling or irresponsible people. It provides a structure for learning to be both loving and in control of one's life and time with others.

After a while, many parents requested another book on boundaries, this one dealing with kids. They said, "I don't want my child to grow up like I did. I want a preventive book on learning about limits." So we wrote *Boundaries with Kids: When to Say Yes, When to Say No to Help Your Children Gain Control of Their Lives* (Zondervan, 1998). This book is not about controlling or making your child behave, which is impossible. It is about structuring his life so that he is free to make choices that will either reward him for responsibility or cause him pain for irresponsibility. As the parent sets appropriate boundaries with the child, the child experiences and internalizes boundaries for himself.

Boundary experiences enlarge the child's ability to be an honest, responsible person. *Your boundaries become the structure that the child must internalize and make his own.* As we show you how to develop responsibility in your child, you may recognize boundary concepts in these ideas because boundaries and responsibility really can't be separated.

The Parent's Task: Love, Truth, Freedom, and Reality

Allison dreaded the after-dinner toy clean-up time with five-year-old Kevin. She and he had done it poorly so many times that it was like a dance with predictable steps:

"Honey, time to clean up your things," Allison says.

Kevin ignores her and keeps playing.

Allison waits a minute or so, then: "Sweetheart, time to clean up, okay?"

Kevin continues to ignore her. (Many kids have told me they are listening to their parent, but are actively seeing how much they can get away with at this point!)

"Kevin, did you hear me?"

"What?"

"I said, clean up!"

"Just a minute."

"Okay, but just one."

Five minutes pass. Then: "Kevin, clean up now!"

"Why?"

"Because it's time to."

"Okay, in a minute."

"No, now!"

"Why?"

"Because I said to! Now, Mister!"

Kevin picks up a toy to put it away and becomes fascinated with it. He sits down and plays with it.

Allison finally becomes psycho-mom: *"If you don't get to work, I'll make you do it, and you'll lose every toy you ever owned, and when I tell your father . . ."*

Kevin knows he's crossed a line with Allison, so he half-heartedly cleans up a few more toys. He now responds to her. But let's look deeper at what really went on. Kevin was able to frustrate and drain Allison. She worked much harder at this than he did. The only reason he started to work was because he didn't like her rage. And the next time he will probably be able to get away with a little more, knowing how to string her along. And maybe he could make it so difficult, she'll throw up her hands and clean the place up herself, muttering, "It's not worth the hassle."

Neither Allison nor Kevin is in control of oneself. Kevin is controlling Allison, not himself. Allison is letting herself be controlled by Kevin, as he masterfully works her. Responsibility is in disarray.

As we have said before, your child is not your ally in learning responsibility. In his mind, he has much to lose and nothing to gain by taking responsibility for his life. But the good news is that he is going to resist responsibility whether you handle it rightly or wrongly. This means that Allison has nothing to lose by approaching her son differently. He will still be passively manipulative to avoid doing his chore—this won't change. However, what he experiences when he tries to manipulate his mom is something Allison has a lot of control over. And this is how kids learn responsibility.

After attending one of our Boundaries with Kids seminars, Allison changed her parenting with Kevin. She told her son that from now on, if he ignored her requests to clean up, she would take away all the toys he had been playing with. The next time Kevin ignored Allison, rather than nagging him, she simply followed through with the consequence she had set. She put away all the toys for a few days. He protested the first few times, but after that, it took only a few seconds for him to clean up when asked.

As your child begins taking responsibility, he shouldn't always be your adversary. God designed him to take responsibility and thus gain freedom. Freedom makes life better. Often, as your child begins experiencing the benefits of responsibility, he becomes a partner in the task (though not without some griping).

Your job in teaching responsibility to your children has four qualities in view: love, truth, freedom, and reality. As you provide these qualities in the right sequences, types, and amounts, you set up a structure for your children that makes irresponsibility painful and responsibility pleasurable. And they grow as responsibility becomes internalized and part of their character structure.

Love

Children learn responsibility only from a loved state. You must forge an emotional alliance with your child before he will develop any sense of responsibility. The child must know that even when you and he disagree, you are "for" him—his welfare, safety, best interests, and growth.

There are two reasons for this. The first is that *responsibility is intricately connected to truth.* Truth is about what exists that is factual; responsibility is our attitude toward what exists.

That is, when we understand truth, then we are responsible to attend to that truth. If you learn about gravity and speed, you need to be responsible not to drive too fast. Like truth, responsibility separates and clarifies realities. For example, in a business, the CEO's and the clerk's responsibilities show that they are separate people with separate tasks.. Responsibility exposes differences between people. This isn't a bad thing. Telling a child to do something he doesn't want to do clarifies the reality that you and your child are two different people, with different agendas and wants in life. Without the bridge of love and attachment between you, your child could feel alienated and isolated from you. There would be no warmth to help him tolerate the differences. Your child needs to know that, though you and he are separate, you are united in safe love.

Second, *responsibility and consequences make your child aware of law and punishment.* Disobeying rules brings a negative experience. By nature, humans are "anti-law," Laws are an offense to the way we want to see life. So we don't want to be exposed to rules and consequences. We always protest this reality at first.

When children first experience law, they don't like it, either. Who in their right mind does? The law is impossible to obey perfectly, yet there's always a penalty involved in falling short of it. The demands of the law make a person angry (Romans 4:15). Children have tantrums, whine, defy authority, or say, "It's not fair." Or they become guilty inside and angrily condemn themselves. For you, the experience is discipline, which teaches. For the child, it is punishment, which judges.

Love is the only way your child can tolerate law in your relationship. Love makes it okay to protest the law but still learn to abide by the rules. And love frees your child from self-judgment when he fails. As Josh McDowell says, "Rules without relationship leads to rebellion."

Empathize with and have compassion for your child's struggle to develop responsible character. His rage, defiance, or whining may be hard on you. But your child is in lots of pain himself—that's why he is protesting. Your child has to give up an entire way of looking at life. His philosophy of "Don't worry, let them do it" is being replaced by, "Worry, it's going to cost you." This is distressing for him.

Begin to integrate grace and truth into your own character as you start helping him take responsibility. Make sure you are doing the attachment work described in the last chapter so that your child will be "rooted and grounded in love" (Ephesians 3:17 NASB). Before you start working on responsibility and boundaries, take the time to develop and cement your love for him.

Give your child grace: "I care deeply for you, even when your attitude makes me angry. And I will be caring deeply for you while you are grounded until your attitude changes." Empathize with his protest against your rules: "I know, honey, having to do homework late at night isn't fun. I hope you'll be okay." These are emotional investments that he can draw on when he hates you or feels you hate him for requiring responsibility. Love bridges the gap that responsibility creates.

Your child may reject you as well as your love when you begin working on responsibility. Kids tend to shoot the messenger of the responsibility lesson. It hurts for a child to hate you, but this is all part of the burden of being a parent. It is a comfort to know that God feels the slings and arrows of his kids every day as they resent, question, blame, and withdraw love from him. But he never removes his love. He knows we need lots of love to learn the lessons of growing up. Stay connected, and keep holding the line with your kid.

Truth

Love is a necessary but insufficient quality to develop character. It is not enough to make the child feel safe and attached. She also needs to know the truths of her responsibilities and duties in life in order to learn, execute, and internalize them. It's hard to hold someone accountable for misbehaving when she hasn't been told the truth: "where there is no law there is no transgression" (Romans 4:15). Truth becomes the structure for her to follow as she learns the rules of life. Children who get clear, age-appropriate boundaries about what is expected are more equipped to respond to the requirements of life.

The "truth" column of the table in chapter 2 is a good overview of what things children can learn to handle at what ages. These are their instructions for life's tasks. Use this as an overall guideline to help structure and direct what you want to help them with. Keep the big picture in mind as you tailor everyday instructions. For example, give your child some chores, but make those chores appropriate to the age of your child. Children between two and four, for example, can help sort laundry. A high school student should be able to cook dinner once a week, while a second-grader can learn how to wash dishes.

If you under-require (expect less than your child can do), you will generally get what you've asked for: underperformance and immaturity. If you over-require (expect more than your child can do), you are likely to get either exasperation (Ephesians 6:4) or discouragement (Colossians 3:21). Your child will be unable to meet your demand.

How you present the truths to your child is important. Here are some ways to convey the rules of life effectively:

- Base rules and expectations on your values. Think and pray about these before you tell them to your child. Go over them with people you trust.
- Be deliberate, not reactive. Don't set guidelines when you are angry.
- Memorialize the rules. Type them up and post them on the refrigerator to prevent the "I didn't know" problem.
- Call a family meeting to let everyone know the rules. Family members will be required to behave, relate, and perform in certain ways.
- Distinguish between universal and specific rules. Universal rules apply to all. Specific rules are problem areas that a particular child is working on. For example, *universally* all the kids in the family are to treat others with respect, while *specifically* Katy needs to work on

not calling people names when she is mad at them. However, the better you construct the universal rules, the fewer specific ones you will need. Just as in writing laws, try to cover the most ground you can, to avoid a million dos and don'ts.

This part requires work. When my (Dr. Townsend's) kids were small, we didn't think about this very much, so we had too many rules. During toothbrushing time in the bathroom, for example, we had the following rules:

1. Don't flick the toothpaste on the mirror.
2. Don't splash each other.
3. Don't spit the goop in the toilet.
4. Don't squeeze toothpaste on the dog.

It was a management nightmare. Finally, we came up with this one universal rule: Leave the bathroom as clean as you found it. A good universal rule is a beautiful thing.

Freedom

Some parents stop with love and truth, thinking that they have taught their child responsibility: "She knows she is loved, and she knows the rules. Now she'll behave." Then they are disappointed or frustrated when their child blithely continues on her way. This is a problem. Love and truth alone don't even work with adults. Why should they work with kids?

Love and truth alone don't teach responsibility. Freedom is at the heart of learning responsibility. Freedom allows your children to experience their choices for themselves. It is not enough to know the rules; your children must also be free to transgress the rules. Helping children with freedom, however, doesn't mean giving them total freedom. You wouldn't let them cross the street to learn the consequences of leaving the yard. When children's safety is at stake, freedom must be curtailed. Consequences need to be painful, but not harmful.

Children need freedom for several reasons.

First, responsibility is impossible without freedom. No one who isn't free to walk away can choose to follow God or you. Your child needs to be free to say no to obeying you. If your child *must* obey, her character is not growing. She may be learning how to play your game, or merely externally complying, but she is not becoming a person of integrity.

Freedom involves the whole person. We are to love God with all our heart, soul, and mind (Matthew 22:37). This unreserved giving over of ourselves to God comes only from a free choice in which we understand the costs and the benefits. In the same way, your child needs the freedom to choose or refuse your ways, so that when she says yes to you, it is with her whole person. The prodigal son's freedom eventually allowed him to repent whole-heartedly and return to his father (Luke 15:11–32).

In fact, freedom is at the heart of our relationship with God. He did not want robots whose love and obedience were guaranteed. This would be meaningless. Instead, he risked all to give us freedom to submit to or reject him. He knew that if we had freedom, choosing him would really matter. Freedom is the price tag of love.

Second, a child needs freedom because love and safety are destroyed without it. A child who is not free to reject your rules is living in fear. If you can force your child to submit to you, it is probably because she is afraid of loss of love, abandonment, attack, and condemnation. This fear cannot coexist with love and loving choices, for "perfect love drives out fear" (1 John 4:18).

Third, a child needs freedom so that if she chooses wrongly and suffers a painful consequence, she will look at herself as the problem, not you. When an outside force controls us, we can externalize blame and responsibility. If I wake up late because a power outage cut off my alarm clock, I have learned very little. If I wake up late because I was tired and didn't set the alarm, I am forced to see myself as the responsible party.

In the same way, your child needs to look at herself as the originator of her choices. If she chooses to come home after curfew and therefore gets grounded, she can't say it's your fault.

She may disagree with the rule, but not her choice. Most likely, if you enforce the consequences, she will tell her friends she needs to get home earlier the next time.

Fourth, a child needs freedom because, as my pastor says all the time about his kids, control is an illusion anyway. We really can't control our friends, spouses, or children. Anyone who thinks he or she can *make* a child do something lives on a different planet. A three-year-old won't eat the beans on her plate until she has reason to. The art of parenting is giving her the right reason.

To tell a child the rules is to assume you are giving her a choice. Truly give her a choice, and let her know she has one. When she says defiantly, "You can't make me," agree completely: "You're right, I certainly can't. *But I can hold off giving you dessert until you freely choose to eat your beans.*"

Reality

This fourth component of developing responsibility is reality, or structuring consequences for the child. We use the word *reality* because parenting needs to mirror the real world as much as possible, to help the child internalize the way things work out there. When an adult is selfish or hurtful, and reality is working right, he loses friends and other good things. Reality, the way God designed it, is your child's friend.

Reality assumes your child will disobey. Testing limits is how a child learns to grow up and take responsibility. Every so often I'll encounter someone at a seminar or on the radio who will ask, "How can I get my child to not cross the boundaries?" The answer is always, "That's her job! Crossing boundaries—testing the limits—is your child's job. Your job is to be on the other side of the crossing and to make it unpleasant for her when she does."

When a child experiences a limit, a loss, or appropriate pain, she begins to internalize the truth that being irresponsible hurts and that being responsible brings good stuff. Bringing reality to bear through consequences helps her take ownership of herself and establish self-control.

Consequences aren't simply to be stated as a threat. Don't set up consequences you aren't willing and able to carry out. Otherwise, your child internalizes the reality, "If I can get past the threats, I can still put off seeing my life as my problem." Following through is everything. Count the cost, and be prepared for much testing of the limits.

To be really effective in this process, you need to set up consequences that have several characteristics. Effective consequences are:

- As close to natural consequences as possible. Refusing food might mean not getting other food until the hated food is eaten, or at least tried.
- Appropriate to the child's developmental maturity level. We don't believe that a sixteen-year-old should get a driver's license by virtue of having a birthday. He has to prove he is mature enough, and he can lose it if he isn't. We also don't believe that a preschooler should automatically watch his favorite TV show just because he understands the story and characters. Parenting helps the child move from demanding rights to earning privileges.
- Appropriately severe. Let the punishment fit the crime. A four-year-old's cranky attitude may bring a time-out. Direct rebellion against Mom might entail removal of favorite toys for some time. For a teen, chronic lateness might mean losing some fun outings. Violence might mean calling the police.
- Administered ASAP. Immediacy allows the child to relate her choice to the consequence with less interference from intervening events over time. For example, you might tell a two-year-old who is having a tantrum in the grocery store that you will take him outside with a consequence. Then follow through right away so that he figures out that bad behavior means unpleasant things.

- Loving. Loss of love *is not* the consequence. The attachment must stay in place (even if the child withdraws her attachment from you). Your being "for" her should not be jeopardized by her behavior. You might say, "You're going to bed early for being wild at dinner, but I do love you, and I want to play with you tomorrow."
- As specific as possible. What will she lose that she loves (or get that she hates), when, and for how long? Vague threats like "You'll be sorry" don't translate well into her experience when she crosses the line.
- Flexible. Change boundaries and consequences as the child takes responsibility and matures. In other words, some boundaries and consequences can be relaxed because the child has internalized them, so you can move on.

These four responsibility builders—love, truth, freedom, and reality—all work together to create a learning and internalizing environment for your child. Generally, as you remain consistent with these four, your child will protest, test, and escalate for a while. When your child sees that you are serious and that you are stronger than she, she will develop the limits for herself.

The Fruits of Responsibility

When *Boundaries with Kids* was released, a friend of mine whose son, Mike, is thirteen years old, said to me, "Mike says he used to like you but not since you wrote this book." I couldn't blame Mike. I remember how I felt at that age. So while you are training your child in responsibility, don't wait for him to rise up and call you blessed.

However, some things you can expect, observe, and encourage in your child as character develops. These things build on each other as he safely takes in the realities you are providing. You will observe this happening at almost any age as the child begins "getting it."

Ownership

Your child's orientation toward life begins to change. To take care of his problems, he looks less to you and more to himself. He still needs lots of love and connection, but he begins to take stewardship of his behavior, attitudes, and emotions. For example, a preschooler girl who always comes to Mom for every rift in her friendships starts dealing better on her own with the ups and downs of relationships.

Self-Control

Ownership leads to self-control, a fruit of the Spirit (Galatians 5:22–23). As your child experiences consistent, appropriate consequences, he takes in the structure. This structure helps him work through impulse problems, procrastination, lack of concentration, temper tantrums, and much more. He becomes more confident and less dependent on you.

There are probably few greater satisfactions to a parent than hearing that his child did a good thing with no one looking over her shoulder. I had a friend who told me that he overheard his teenage daughter on the phone refusing to go to a party because there would be drugs there. Although she was being pressured by her girlfriend, she stuck to her guns, simply because her values were more important than peer pressure.

Freedom

As your child develops self-control, he creates the space in his head to think maturely about his choices. Self-control helps him take stock of what he should and shouldn't do. This is a different freedom than you give the child in establishing consequences. That freedom is a gift from you, to help the child learn. This freedom, however, does not come from the parent. It is the ability—which the child earns and develops over time—to make good, value-based decisions. The parent provides the first freedom, which is the freedom to fail and learn. The child then develops the second freedom, which is the ability to say no to himself, based on your love, freedom, and consequences.

It is your child's freedom from bondage to childlike things such as his impulses, intense emotions, peer pressure, and pleasure-based thinking.

On a drive to buy clothes, a young girl may ask her mom to take a side trip to the local toy store. When Mom refuses, the girl feels sad for a few seconds, then begins talking about the clothing store. She is free to respond to her mom, and not bound to a childish demand that she get her way all the time.

This earned freedom gives your child a foundation from which to make moral, relational, and spiritual decisions. She is truly able to make her own choices: "But if serving the LORD seems undesirable to you, then choose for yourselves this day whom you will serve, whether the gods your forefathers served beyond the River, or the gods of the Amorites, in whose land you are living. But as for me and my household, we will serve the LORD" (Joshua 24:15). A free child has learned the blessings of owning and choosing well.

The Motive Issue

Some parents worry about a child's motives at this point. They don't want their child to grow simply based on a fear of consequences. They want their child to want to do the right thing because it is the right thing. They fear that a kid who is only afraid of consequences will grow up to be an adult whose only reason for obeying laws and staying true in marriage is a fear of getting caught. This is not a mature person, nor one whose motives are ruled by love, which is the highest motive: "This is my command: Love each other" (John 15:17). Parents want a child who grows up to be responsible and faithful because he cares and wants to do the right thing.

This is a valid concern. If child rearing were only about helping children to be good to avoid pain, we would not be doing a great job of instilling the image of God. God is more interested in love than he is in being comfortable. In fact, his love for us sometimes causes him great pain (Hosea 11:8). However, a couple of principles about motives can help clarify the issue.

First, *motives are developmental.* Children learn obedience at different levels of complexity. They start life off as lawless and self-centered individuals. They have little ability to empathize with their mother's exhaustion and discomfort as she takes care of them. Gradually, they experience rules and prohibitions as well as the pain associated with doing the wrong things. Bad things happen when rules are broken. Good things happen when rules are followed.

Then come more advanced reasons to behave righteously, such as morality, learning universal codes of conduct and ethics, and empathy for others. We will deal with these in chapter 8 in the section on conscience. But these qualities are based on lovingly structuring the child's early reality so that he understands that life is better for him when he is responsible. So hang on—he probably will develop more "pure" motives to do right.

Second, though altruism and love of God are the highest motives, *none of us are mature enough to only be driven by these*. Therefore it is a good thing that while we strive to become people who are driven by love, the other realities are still in operation as a spiritual check-and-balance system. This protects us against our fallenness, immaturity, and lapses into selfishness.

For example, a man may be tempted to fudge on a business deal. To help him stay righteous, he may remember that he answers to God, or that he wouldn't want to be cheated on. Now, if these higher motives fail and he's had a bad day and feels entitled to special treatment from the world, it is good for him to remember that losing his job, paying fines, and perhaps going to jail are things he doesn't want. This man's condition is not much different from that of you and your child: you both love and care, but you both have a wayward part that needs to know about reality.

Attachment and responsibility form much of a child's character. Next we will deal with how to help him solve a problem as old as humankind: dealing with the reality of imperfection.

Six

Living in an Imperfect World

Reality

I remember the day a mother at a seminar on "Raising Successful Kids" asked me, "Dr. Cloud, what is the best thing parents can teach their child?"

It surprised me how quickly an answer came to mind. "I don't know whether there's 'one best thing.' But I can tell you one that's way up there on the list."

"What's that?" she asked, probably expecting a spiritual pillar of character such as love, righteousness, faith, hope, perseverance, or obedience.

"Teach your child how to lose."

"What?"

"I said, 'Teach him how to lose.'"

"What do you mean, 'Teach him how to lose?' I want my child to win. Why on earth would you want to teach your child how to lose?"

I just looked at her and said, "Because he will lose. And since he will, he'd better know how."

Because he will lose. These words are not only the most important ones of this interaction, but also the most difficult ones for any parent to hear. We don't like to lose. But in reality, we all do. And what ultimately separates the winners from the losers is not that winners lose less. *It is that they lose better.* Losing well, with the ability to continue on, is one of the most important character traits you can develop in your child.

The Lost Ideal

Along with this mother, you may be wondering, "Why teach children to lose?" And what does losing have to do with "reality"—the topic of this chapter? The answer is that reality is a place where things do not always go as we would like. When we fail, or when circumstances or relationships do not turn out as we had hoped, we have to keep going and try to make the best of a bad situation. Your child's ability to do this will determine how well his life goes.

Has your child ever experienced the "lost ideal"—the reality we are no longer living in Paradise, but in an imperfect world—in any of the following ways?

Screams of aloneness or hunger
Banging one's head on the coffee table
A scream of anger when hearing no
Terror and rage when you go out for the evening
Sadness at not getting picked for the playground softball team
Feelings of rejection when not invited to Susie's birthday party
Feelings of shame and guilt when punished
Getting a bad grade in school after trying hard
Not being good enough to make the soccer team
Hatred of discipline and a loss of privileges
Resentment at limits and rules
Betrayal by a friend
Anger at not being allowed to go out when one wants
Practicing hard for the big part in the school play and not getting it
Being on the wrong end of a breakup
The death of a friend or loved one

The list could go on. As a friend of mine says to her young son, "Livin's hard." Your job is to make the hard job of living no more difficult than it has to be. You can do this by building character into your child that is able to overcome the pain and loss that everyone encounters.

The Real Loss

In the real world, the one where we all have to live, we experience a conflict between how things should be and how they really are. It all started in the Garden of Eden, when God created everything "good." The world was a place of blessings, not curses. Life was as it should be. Then we fell from paradise, were locked out of the Garden, and encountered a less-than-perfect world, a world of sin and loss. As Jesus said, "In the world you have tribulation" (John 16:33 NASB). Almost every day, in some form or another, your children will find this to be true.

But because they were created for Eden, not a fallen world, your children still wish for things to be perfect and ideal. In fact, sometimes life can approximate perfection, when we encounter love or see a beautiful piece of work well done. But even these moments of perfection coexist with sin and failure. Learning to accept both the good and the bad enables your children to have a firm grounding in reality and to create a life that will help them pursue what's left of Eden without giving up along the way.

The Three Realities

In this "world of tribulation," your children, from the beginning of life, are going to have to learn to overcome imperfection in three spheres:

Self
Other people
The world

Self

When I was a sophomore in college, I volunteered to be a "sophomore advisor." In my freshman year, my sophomore advisors were great to me, and I wanted to pass it on. SA's, as we were called, lived on the freshman floors of the dorms and helped freshmen adapt to college life. We gained some basic training in crisis management and listening skills.

One day I came back from class about lunchtime to the sounds of sobbing down the hall. The sounds were coming from Matt's room. His door was open a crack, and as I walked closer, I could hear him talking to his mother on the telephone. His mother appeared to be consoling him because of the grade he had received on one of his freshman English papers.

As they talked, I could hear him move from despair to hopefulness. He sounded as if he was agreeing with his mom. When he hung up, I went in, and we talked. Matt had indeed gotten a bad grade, which he had not been used to in high school, and his mother had "helped" him by agreeing with him that the teacher was just not good enough to recognize good work when she saw it. With her "liberal East Coast training," the teacher could not appreciate his more conservative views. He felt better and was ready to play some basketball. I was ready to throw up.

His mother had totally shielded Matt from the reality of his failure by blaming the teacher and making him believe that he was still "the best." It was sickening.

I have had the opportunity to follow Matt and his family through the years, and the story has been the same. In Matt's family there is no such thing as failure. When something goes wrong, it's always "somebody else's fault." He and his three brothers have had a history of failures, but they never seem to learn from them.

The first reality your children will have to learn to face is this: *They are not ideal or perfect.* They are flawed, imperfect people who will fail, lose, and make mistakes. From somewhere in the second year of life on throughout development, this reality presents itself over and over again. If they can handle it, children will be able to overcome those flaws and imperfections. But if they can't, they will be like Matt. Each time they will be surprised that the world did not reflect their perfection.

When I got to know the family, I understood why it was that way. Mom and Dad had a lot invested in the children being the "perfect" kids, reflecting the "perfect" family. But the perfect family does not teach children how to be imperfect. So it ends up with many surprises when things do not go as planned.

Your children need to know that they are not perfect.

Other People

Your children also need to learn that other people are not perfect. They wish that they were all perfect, which usually translates to "Don't cause me grief." They want others to gratify them, to never make mistakes, and certainly to never hurt them. This is how Eden was!

In reality, though, they will find a whole gamut of people out there. Some are basically good and fair; others are not. What will your children do? Will they be prepared? Will they be able to spot the good ones and avoid the destructive ones? And will the good ones be good enough for them when they are less than perfect? You will have to prepare your children to deal with all of these questions. The risks are twofold: raising a "brat," on one end of the spectrum, who demands that everyone be just what she wants them to be, and a "codependent," on the other end, who tolerates destructive behavior from everyone.

Kerri brought her seven-year-old son, Andy, in for counseling because he was beginning to have problems with his relationships at school. In fact, he didn't have any relationships— at least, none that lasted very long. As soon as one of his friends frustrated him in some way, he would just leave and not want to play with him any more. He would get so frustrated, he couldn't work out the conflict. He had the same problem at home with his two sisters. He couldn't tolerate people making mistakes.

In children we see this pattern in play. Later in life, we see perfectionistic demands on coworkers, spouses, and friends. Learning to live with imperfect people is an important character trait to have.

The World

Not only will your children frustrate themselves and be frustrated by others, but the world will frustrate them as well. Birthday parties will get rained out. Pets will die. Toys will break, and bicycles will get stolen. In short, they will experience—in a thousand ways—the lost ideal of not living in Eden. They will have many days in which very frustrating things will happen.

But so do all the happy people in the world. Your job is to help your children develop the character that will enable them to be happy in a world that daily gives them opportunity to be miserable. How to do this is the subject of this chapter. This chapter will teach you how to develop character in your child to overcome losses, failure, sin, and evil, in themselves, in others and in the world around them. Then they can truly be the kind of people Jesus commanded to "take courage; I have overcome the world" (John 16:33 NASB).

The Problem Defined

In short, the problem is this: God created your children to live in a perfect world, with perfect others, and to be perfect themselves. But now, in a fallen world, they have to live with both the ideals and the imperfection. Your task is to teach them to hold on to and pursue their ideals while accepting, forgiving, and redeeming the imperfection they encounter in themselves, others, and the world around them. To do this, you will have to give them the character to face reality, to handle it with grace, and to overcome it.

Your children will bring into the world the tendency to split their experience into "all good" or "all bad" feelings and judgments. They will naturally, like all of us, see themselves and others as "good" when things go well, or as "bad" when things don't. In infancy, you can see this in the rage with which babies view you when you can't always foresee and prevent their getting hungry or being alone. They experience you as the "all-bad Mommy" or the "all-bad Daddy."

In toddlerhood, children experience you as the "all-bad" parent who sets limits on them and frustrates their wish to be in control. In early childhood, they judge themselves harshly when they are not able to perform as they would like. Later, traumatized adolescents who do not get asked to the prom the first week see themselves as "total dorks," or "losers."

Only the internalized character of grace and truth can help children negotiate life's ups and downs successfully. And that character can only come from many experiences with a loving but truthful parent who forces them to deal with reality, accept themselves and others, and continue on to pursue their ideals.

Fig Leaves for Everyone

When something goes wrong in life, whether inside or outside of us, a predictable natural strategy is set into motion. This strategy is to make sure that neither we nor anyone else knows the truth. We have many names for this strategy, from denial to defense mechanisms to good old-fashioned lying and covering up. These strategies all fulfill the same purpose of keeping the pain or badness out of our own or someone else's awareness.

In the Bible, this strategy is symbolized by Adam and Eve's fig leaves. Adam and Eve hid from the truth, and they hid from God because they were afraid (Genesis 3:10). As Adam said, he was afraid to be naked and exposed. We are all just like Adam. We are afraid to be naked and exposed in the reality of who we are with our pain, failure, sin, or brokenness. So we have ways of hiding from this reality, as do your children. Let's look at how the fig leaves operate in the parenting process and what you should avoid.

You should be aware of four barriers to helping your child deal with reality: denial of the bad things, denial of the ideals, judgment of the bad, and lack of experience of the bad things in life. These are seen in every age and stage of life.

Denial of the Bad

In the example given above, we can see that Matt and his mother denied the bad. Neither could face the fact that Matt did not have strong enough English composition skills. For him, it was academics. For others, it's relationships. For still others, it's activities. Parents tend to deny that their child is the problem, and they shift the problem to some outside agency.

The other day I talked to a parent who was berating her son's soccer coach. Her son had not made the team, and she went on and on about how crummy the coach was and how blind he was to her son's skills.

In reality, her son was just not good enough. His not making the soccer team had more to do with her husband's lack of involvement with his son than the coach's blindness. But to face the conflict with her husband was much more scary than to blame the coach. In shifting the blame, however, she was training her son to believe he was not the one who needed to improve.

Some parents are so in denial of their children's problems that they place them in life-and-death danger, as in the case of severe eating disorders. "Certainly you can't be saying that Susie's problem is anything but physical," they say. It is much easier for them to think that Susie has a poor metabolism than it is to think she needs to grow emotionally. Life-and-death eating disorders are the extreme, but subtle denial of children's problems or faults is very common in many parents' day-to-day parenting.

Children readily deny their own sin and problems as well. I was visiting friends not long ago when their four-year-old, playing where he was not supposed to, knocked over a cabinet of very fragile belongings. I watched him sneak out, thinking that he had not been detected. Seeing his planned escape, I chuckled to myself.

"Jeffrey, what are you up to?" I asked him.

He looked up and forced a smile. "Oh, nothing! Nothing at all!" He quickly ran outside.

I was amused at his childlike denial of what he had done, thinking that he could get away with it if no one knew. Fortunately, his parents were skilled in helping him to face his mistakes. Because of that, he will learn.

Denial of the Ideals

The other way to deal with the tension of living in both the good and the bad is to deny the ideal altogether. Some parents label their children as "bad" when they do not live up to their expectations. How many times have you heard parents refer to one of their children as the "black sheep of the family"? These parents have given up hope that their child can actually do anything right and have assigned him the role of the "bad one."

Other parents do not go to the extreme of labeling their child, but their tone of voice when correcting her is so "all bad" that the child perceives herself as a loser or an "all-bad" person. This affects her self-concept in such a way that she sees herself as "bad" when she fails, instead of seeing her behavior as a problem to be dealt with.

Still other parents maintain this split between good and bad by not being involved enough with their child or by not pushing their child to perform in reasonable ways. A child who is not forced to face his imperfections never resolves the "good me–bad me" split inside. Since the split is only resolved through failure, the child who is not disciplined, corrected, and forgiven never learns to push toward the ideal and handle failure. Children who supposedly "have it easy," in reality, don't have it easy at all. They are left with an unintegrated self-concept; they never find out that they are not as good as they think they are. Maintain high ideals of character for your children and require them to attain them. In the process of failure and correction, they become whole.

The same is true for performance expectations. Many parents, fearing that they will damage the child's self-concept, shy away from performance expectations. Expectations never hurt anyone. On the contrary, they shape and form character. Dealing with our failure to meet expectations is part of the process that integrates us. Problems come when you do not expect (and then correct for) failure, when your expectations are unrealistic, or when you do not correct with grace and forgiveness. You don't do your children any favors by denying the need for them to perform to standards of goodness or excellence. They need to have academic standards, or other performance standards, for example. They will have them for the rest of their lives. Do not deny the good, either in the child or in the standard itself.

Judgment of the Bad

Another dynamic that interferes with a child's integrating the good and the bad is what the Bible refers to as "judgment." Judgment is the condemning emotional tone with which imperfection is met. Judgment is reflected in such things as wrath, guilt, loss of love, and condemnation. In parenting we usually see judgment as anger and crippling guilt messages toward failure. While we will deal with the dynamic of judgment more completely in the chapter on conscience, we mention it here because judgment will keep a child from facing reality.

To the extent that children are afraid that their imperfections will cost them love or will incur anger or crippling guilt, they will be afraid to be forthcoming with their failures. They will hide the bad (using whatever fig leaf is available) to keep from being found out. No one wants to show his failure if he thinks that someone will no longer love him or will condemn him. Judgment, or wrathful shame and condemnation, is one of the key barriers to children being able to integrate their "bad parts." If, for example, Joey is struggling with temptation, but is afraid of judgment, he is more apt to hide the problem. Good advice for parents comes from the Bible: "Get rid of all bitterness, rage and anger, brawling and slander, along with every form of malice. Be kind and compassionate to one another, forgiving each other, just as in Christ God forgave you" (Ephesians 4:31–32).

Lack of Experience

Another barrier some children face is the lack of experience in failure. This results when parents do not give their children the opportunity to fail. The parents are so overprotective that the children can't "blow it." They don't have the opportunity to find out that they can't do everything they thought they could. Appropriate risk-taking and freedom to attempt new skills give children the chance to find out that they do not know everything, nor do they know how to do everything. New experiences humble us.

When I was a senior in high school, my parents let me drive two hundred miles away to a golf tournament with a few friends. It was a big step. I was definitely past anything I had every been allowed to do before. But, my parents figured that I was a year away from college, and this would be good practice. Well, it was.

Disaster hit. Our car broke down at night on the Lake Ponchatrain Bridge in New Orleans. We were stranded for six hours trying to get a tow truck and a garage open late at night. In addition, we had to find a way to pay without the necessary cash. What a tough experience it was for a bunch of kids! But, what an experience in learning that we did not know everything and that there really are tough realities to face when you are "on your own."

The Myth of "Positive Self-Esteem"

There is a lot of talk today about self-esteem. Parents are careful to build it in their children. People seek it for themselves. Therapists encourage it in their clients. Does it help? Can you build it? What is it you are trying to build when you build "self-esteem"?

People who talk about building positive self-esteem in a child are often trying to cure the child from the feeling of "bad self" we have talked about above. Or, they are trying to prevent the child from developing a "bad self" in the first place by having the child see himself solely in a positive light. This is a confusing idea for several reasons.

First, it places the security of the child at risk by basing it on her positive performance. The concept of self-esteem hinges on a child's being able to see herself positively. What happens when her performance is not positive? What happens when she fails?

If the goal is to see ourselves in a "good" way, what will we do with failure? Hide it? Explain it away? Rationalize it? Deny it? How can we maintain this "positive view" in the light of sin, badness, and failure? One answer is to have more positive than negative. Another is to have others always building us up. None of these answers ends up with the only security that protects us from any possible failure: love.

A better way than seeing ourselves as *good* is seeing ourselves as *loved*. A child who is loved as herself, both good and bad, does not need to see herself as positive or negative. She sees herself as loved, and the whole issue goes away. A loved self is stronger than a positive self; the child doesn't need to worry about losing her "good self." She doesn't need to hide or deny what she does. No matter how she performs, she will be loved.

A second problem with self-esteem is that the focus is on maintaining a good view of ourselves as opposed to maintaining relationship. Happy people do not get all caught up in themselves. They do not get obsessed with whether or not they are "good enough." They focus more on tasks and loving other people. When they fail, they try to solve the problem. They don't worry about their "goodness." They are more into learning how to do better.

The self-esteem problem is a false solution to a wrong focus. Think of the people you know who are unhappy. Many of them perform as well as those who are much happier. The difference is that the unhappy ones are always worried about not being "good enough," and the happy ones don't even think in those terms. The latter are more into others and life itself.

A third problem with focusing on self-esteem is that the "good self" is a proud self. And a proud self does not develop the kind of humility before God and others that results in gratitude. We are grateful because we find love and success beyond what we deserve. It is all grace. As the Bible says, we don't have anything that wasn't first given to us (1 Corinthians 4:7). So even our talents should lead us to have gratitude toward the God who gave them. The "good self" does not focus on the "good Giver." In reality, self-esteem is a result of being the beneficiary of love.

We are not advocating a return to "worm theology," where people are seen as lowly sinners only. Seeing ourselves as only dirty rotten sinners is just as unhelpful as seeing ourselves as faultless saints. Everyone is created in God's image and has incredible value to him. We are both image bearers and sinners. We are beautiful at times and not so pretty at other times. The real question is where the safety comes from that allows us to be all that we are. And the Bible's answer to that is love. "There is no fear in love. But perfect love drives out fear, because fear has to do with punishment. The one who fears is not made perfect in love" (1 John 4:18).

Nor are we saying that children should not be praised for doing well. Praise is a great motivator. Validating his ability to do something consolidates a child's feeling of competency. The parental stamp of approval helps the child internalize this feeling of competency. Children were created with a need for parental approval, so praise them for a job well done. This does not create pride. Praise is a good thing. Validate your children's talents and abilities. Fill up their tummies with good feelings about themselves. It is important for children to feel good and secure about their talents, work, and abilities.

But do not buy in to the philosophy that building positive self-esteem is the answer to all of the child's problems. Doing so creates more problems than it solves. One of the groups that tests highest in self-esteem is federal prisoners! Obviously, self-esteem failed to develop character in that group. Children need, most of all, to feel loved as they are, and then to be encouraged to learn how to do things well from a loved position. The issue of "Am I good enough?" will become a non-issue. A "loved self" is much more secure than a "good self" any day.

The Cure: Safe Enough to Be Real

Making children feel bad does not motivate them to do better. Nor does making them feel good guard them from all of life's pitfalls. The answer to the self-esteem problem is this: Give them a combination of grace and truth, and they will feel safe enough to be real. The cure to the problem of self-image, self-concept, and self-esteem is to have enough grace to be who one really is.

Your children need, above all, to develop a "real" self. They need enough grace to face and bring into relationship who they really are at any given moment. They need to know that it is okay to fail, to hurt, or to be less than perfect. They need to feel secure in bringing their bad parts to relationship.

If they can be real, their pains and problems can be cured. There is no problem that the grace and guidance of a loving parent cannot get them through. But if they do not feel that they can be who they really are, then their problems never get solved. They just get hidden away to grow into bigger cancers.

The Process of Embracing Reality

How do you teach children to live in an imperfect world? You start by forcing them to face reality and by giving them enough grace to embrace reality and move on. Let's take a closer look at this process.

Protest

When reality hits us, we all respond predictably: we hate it! The first thing we do is protest. We say, "No! It can't be." Recently, a friend of mine died. When he died, his wife screamed, "No! No! No!" This is a natural response to an awful thing. Life should not be this way. Pain should not exist. And the natural human response is to protest the reality.

A child is no different. The first thing a child will do is protest the painful reality. If he experiences the pain of separation, he will scream for his parent. If he experiences the pain of discipline, he will protest the limit. If he experiences the pain of failure, he will protest the reality, saying things like, "I should have done better." Anything but acceptance is the first response.

Reality Remains

The next phase in the process is that the reality remains. If his protest does not change something, the child must finally deal with the reality as being real. It is at this point that much discipline falters. The parent sets the limit, the child protests, and the parent relents. For a limit to be accepted and dealt with, it must remain. In the story of Matt, the reality of his not being a good enough writer to get a good grade did not remain, so he could not grow. His mother explained this reality away. So he did not have to change at all.

But good parents, the kind who help their children live in reality and grow, let the reality remain so that their children can learn to deal with it. Parents who rush in to change painful realities for their children aren't doing them any favors. They teach their children that pain is not really a part of life and that someone will always fix it for them. When Mom or Dad is not around, such a child may turn to drugs to do away with the pain instead of dealing with it. Let failure, discipline, or loss be what it is. Let reality remain when it is truly reality. If the child can solve the problem, wonderful. If he can undo his failure, great. But ultimately what is true is true.

Metabolize the Reality

The next step is that the child learns that the protest is not going to change the reality and that they must metabolize the reality. You may remember from tenth-grade biology how metabolism works. Metabolism refers to the chemical and physical changes that go on continually in your body. To vastly simplify, you take food in, turn what is good into energy, and get rid of the rest. Thus, the child must face the reality, learn from it, and move on. He must take the good from the experience and let go of the bad.

An example would be trying out for the soccer team. He did not make it and was very sad. Empathize, but don't rescue. Talk about it. What did he learn? Help him value the fun he had in trying, and also to accept the sadness in failing. But at the same time, there is a good lesson to be taken forward: "I need to practice and develop more skills in order to make it next year." There is a good lesson to be kept even in a bad experience.

The only way children can accept painful reality is through love. They need enough love to let it go. They experience this love through empathy. The soothing words of a mother or father make children feel safe enough to accept the difficult reality of whatever they have lost: "I know, honey, I know. It's so painful to have to miss the movie with your friends because you didn't get your chores done." Empathy, which is grace communicated, makes living on this side of Eden okay. It validates the pain of the child and makes a bridge back to love. It takes the sting out of what they have lost.

Grief

If you empathize with your children's loss, hurt, or failure, they can face the reality of the loss and then grieve and let go of whatever was valued and is gone. They may have to let go of the wish to have won instead of losing. They may have to let go of a lost love. They may have to humbly realize that they don't have a talent that they wish they had. They may have to let go of the hurt from an injury suffered at the hands of another child. But whatever the hurt, with enough reality and empathy, children will mourn and let it go.

And this is the only way to be comforted. As Jesus said, "Blessed are those who mourn, for they will be comforted" (Matthew 5:4). Those who mourn get comforted, and then they are able to go on.

This is why I told the mother at the seminar that one of the best things she could teach her child was to lose well. If a child can face his losses, he can get comforted and go on. But there is no comfort for the one who continually protests a reality that's never going to change. Losing well means moving into a state of comfort. This is blessed indeed.

Problem Solving and Resolution

The next stage is solving the problem. When we fail at a task or don't reach a goal, we need to learn why we failed and try again.

I grew up as a competitive golfer, and I went through this cycle many times. When I would lose a tournament, I would be angry. I would protest vehemently. But the score would remain, and my teacher would comfort me with his wisdom. He would help me understand that everyone loses sometimes. It was a natural part of sports. Through his comfort and that of others, I would be sad, and let it go. But resolution was on its way! At six o'clock the next morning you could find me on the practice range trying to overcome whatever fault it was that caused me to lose the tournament. And that is how we grow.

Resolution involves finding out what we did wrong, fixing it to the extent possible, and in any case, continuing on. Resolution builds perseverance and achieves goals.

In relationships, problem solving means forgiving and reconciling. If your child has been the offender and he has been disciplined, then resolution might be repenting, apologizing to the one whom he offended, and asking for forgiveness. If he has been the offended one, then he must confront the problem and offer forgiveness to the person who offended him.

In both areas of life, performance and relationship, the path is the same. After the pain has been processed through facing reality, receiving comfort, and grieving, then we must push on to the next step. In the area of performance, it is "get back on the horse and try again." In the area of relationship, it is "confront, repent, forgive, and reconcile." In either side of life, God's goal is for us to keep going. Neither pain nor sin nor failure nor anything else can stop us if we have reality, comfort, the ability to grieve, and the courage to go on. Our God is one who brings forth victory from any defeat. And if we lose well, we can be victorious, too.

This is one of the best lessons your child can ever learn. There is no loss in life great enough that facing the truth with grace and having the courage to go forward cannot cure. That is the formula for happiness.

Some Examples

In the various stages of childhood, the formula is the same, but the content changes.

Infancy

Loss is not something infants have to learn. They are born into it. They are born separated from love and truth; they have no love and security inside them. So they do not need to be given reality. It is there from day one.

The above process goes like this for an infant:

Pain→Comfort→Internalize Comfort Until Next Pain→
Pain→Comfort→Internalize Comfort Until Next Pain→
and so on.

Limits are inherent in infants. Separation is a reality because they have not internalized love inside. The hunger and need states of infants are so overwhelming they must be transformed by comfort and love. You do not have to teach infants not to be selfish. You must satisfy and comfort their needs first. This will build up their experience of the "good" that will have the power to metabolize the "bad."

That is why *you cannot spoil an infant*. Spoiling means causing someone to avoid independence and responsibility. Infants are born cut off from love and unable to take responsibility. The Bible's word for *wean* means to "deal bountifully with." Give comfort to your infant so that she can learn to internalize the care and empathy that will help her to accept reality later. The constant cycle from pain to comfort lays the foundation for a child to learn to put good and bad experience together. It actually builds brain structures that will enable infants to soothe themselves later. If you allow them to have prolonged, overwhelmingly painful experiences of terror without comforting them, they will not have the internal neurological equipment to metabolize the bad experience inside of them. This ability to metabolize bad experience is completely achieved later if you lay down the foundation of comfort early in infancy.

People who say that infants are trying to manipulate you and need to be taught not to be selfish do not understand the absence of thought processes in babies. Babies do not even have the brain capacity to think that way. They are just in despair and need to be comforted. These stages are the foundation of their learning that grace can overcome painful reality. Love them out of their distress.

Toddlerhood

Toddlers go through the process as you give them limits, and they encounter the limits of their own abilities. They hit reality, maybe a no from Mommy. They protest. You hold the limit. They move into more rage and then finally give in to a sadness you can comfort. Give them empathy while you keep the limit, and they learn to lose something they need to lose now: the wish to be God. Toddlers need to learn that they are not in control of the universe; it is a difficult loss to go through. Give them enough limits to find that out, and enough empathy to grieve it. Then get them moving to resolution by pushing them back out there to find out that the next task is still fun even if they lost the last control battle.

Early Childhood

In early childhood and school-age years, as we have said before, skills, morals, and relationships become very important. In every area, give your children a limit or let them experience it for themselves. Then let it stay. Don't rescue them from it. Let them be angry, and let that anger give way to acceptance.

If the situation involves relationships and your child is in the wrong, require him to go to the person, apologize, and make amends. Teach him to ask for forgiveness. If he has been wronged, don't rescue him from the process. Don't listen to his blame and whining about his sister, brother, or friend. Tell him to go tell the person, work it out, and forgive. This is a skill he will need for the rest of his life. And do this with him yourself. One of the best things a child can learn is that working out conflict is a good thing.

In tasks and skills, give your children opportunities to fail. Correct them, but limit the blame and protest. Give them grace to fail, but have them accept the reality of their performance and work on it. Don't allow quitting unless there is a good reason. Overcoming difficulty and failure builds perseverance. Accept only finished work in chores and tasks. Require your children to complete the projects they have begun.

In terms of moral issues, give your children the standards and also the safety to talk about the parts of themselves that are not up to the standard. If you do not allow them to express "bad parts" appropriately, they will develop a bad side that will act out or be afraid. Give them the safety to talk about their hatred, anger, and selfishness. But teach them what to do with those feelings. You don't have to punish them or deny them. "We all have bad feelings, but you are forgiven for feeling that way. Now, even though you are feeling like you hate your sister, what are you going to do?"

Confession and understanding give children the safety to own their feelings and find someone to help them resolve them constructively. If children feel safe to talk about feelings that they know are not good, they do not fear them and they learn to deal with destructive feelings in a positive way. That way they do not develop the "good-bad split," which is being nice on the outside and full of hatred on the inside.

A problem in many Christian homes is that children aren't free to bring the "less than perfect" part of themselves into the light. They feel as though they have to always be "good" and that their bad parts have no place. So, the good-bad split develops with the good on the outside and the bad stuff on the inside in the darkness of their souls. Then, either they act out and rebel, or they pick destructive friends or lovers to act out the bad side for them. Give them the safety to show their less than perfect feelings so they can integrate them while they are in relationship with you. This prevents them from hiding their feelings from you and maintaining the split inside of themselves.

Adolescence

In adolescence, the good-bad split gets reawakened. Adolescents test out new aspects of themselves. Dating is a whole new world that will have to run the roller-coaster ride of "Am I good enough?" So, as your adolescents go through all of those experiences, be there to process the pain and the victories. Don't be surprised at the up-and-down nature of it all.

In addition, make sure that they have a safe place to process their feelings. You will be able to provide some of that, but not all. Youth pastors and counselors are very important for this reason. Adolescents are feeling a lot that they need to integrate, including feelings toward you. Some of their struggle may be sexual. Inasmuch as it is possible, make it safe for them to talk to you. But give them other places to integrate as well.

Limits help with integration—if you hold to them. As you hold to appropriate rules and limits, they will hate you on the one hand for thwarting their desires and love you on the other for the safety you provide. Not getting caught up in power struggles will help your teenagers to integrate all that they feel about limits. If you do not get controlling or aggressive, they will be able to internalize your limits.

Being Hated

One of most important qualities for a parent to possess to integrate their children is *the ability to be hated*. It sounds strange, but your child will never integrate their good and bad feelings if you are uncomfortable with their anger toward you. Their protest is absolutely essential for the process, and if you get scared of their anger and remove the limit, integration cannot take place. This is why codependent parents create codependent children. You must allow them to get angry and frustrated with you.

On the other hand, if you get angry in return, that keeps the split going as well. The answer is to remain firm with the limit, and empathize. "I know you hate me. I know you hate that you cannot go. But that's how it is. I'm sorry it's so upsetting to you." These kinds of nonreactive but firm responses keep the child from getting you into a power struggle whereby they can avoid the process of acceptance and grief. If you hold firm—and provide the empathy and the love we talked about earlier—the process can unfold. Your children can move through the process from protest to grief to acceptance. But only if you are firm.

The Result

If all of this goes well, you will have built several things into your children's character that will last them a lifetime. They will have the ability to:

- Be real and honest about who they are
- Let go of failures and losses
- Forgive and be forgiven
- Reconcile with others
- Face failures and learn from them
- Solve problems and persevere
- Enjoy life and the process without the pressure to be "perfect"
- Love people who are real and imperfect themselves
- Hold on to and pursue ideals even when they have not reached them or fail them

These character traits will enable your child to live a good life this side of Eden—not a perfect life, but a good and satisfying one. Every day, inching toward perfection and never getting there, they will enjoy the process. If that is true, you have done a very good job of helping them to live in reality.

In the next chapter, we will look at some of those realities.

Seven

Developing Gifts and Talents

Competence

My sons and I (Dr. Townsend) are members of a father-son group called Indian Guides. Dads and sons get together regularly for sports competitions, camp outs, and outings. One of the major annual events of Indian Guides is a Pinewood Derby.

The Pinewood Derby is a race of six-inch-long cars made from pine. Each father and son must construct their car as a team. They design, saw, sand, install the wheels, weight, and paint the cars together. This process takes many hours. Our local race draws a couple of hundred cars, so there is a high level of competition.

In the derby, little things are big deals. The race itself, monitored by computer, is only a few seconds long. Races are won and lost by hundredths of a second. Because of this, people over the years have studied the nuances of derby car construction to shave milliseconds off their time. For example, there are certain ways to make a car run with less friction. I recently found eleven derby construction sites on the Internet, all dealing with tips on making one's car faster. The level of technical information about derbies is now so sophisticated that you have to work at having fun while building a topflight car. Our local tribe has the perfect balance in this tension.

One of the boys, Ryan, who is ten, has become a derby expert. Over the years his dad, Jim, has gradually handed off more and more responsibility to Ryan in building their race car. Ryan has won three citywide championships in a row. This past year a group of dads and sons met in Jim's garage to work on our derby cars for the upcoming race. Jim offered to give us some pointers on making a winning car. We assembled with our kits and tools, then Jim looked over at his son and said, "Ryan, take it away."

Ryan stood up and quietly explained body design, sanding, wheel polishing, and axle positioning. He gave examples and showed alternatives. In short, he did a great job. I was impressed with his command of the subject. It reminded me a little of Jesus in the temple (Luke 2:46). And I followed his instructions. My son, Ricky, and I didn't win big, but we were faster this year than last! (Yes, I admit it: I wanted not only fun, but also victory.)

At ten, Ryan not only has mastered derby construction, but is training adults in it. I doubt that, when he grows up, Ryan will race derby cars full-time. But he is well on his way to taking his place in the workforce in a few years, equipped to excel.

Your Child Is a Working Child

Even when he is young, your child has to work. Work is a central aspect of our existence. Much of the time and energy invested in living involves some work, such as:

- Career
- Life skills (hygiene, clothing, finances, time management, and home maintenance)
- School
- Sports
- Technical hobbies
- Training

God designed us not only to be in relationship and to connect, but to be productive in the world, to contribute meaningfully to others in a significant way. Part of Adam and Eve's job description was subduing and ruling the world (Genesis 1:28), and that task has been handed down to us through the centuries.

Competence is the area of character growth we will be discussing in this chapter. We will tell you how you can help your children develop the capacity to be experts in some area, to perform well as craftspeople, and to contribute meaningfully through their gifts and abilities. Children who grow up competent in something are better able to function in the adult world, where expertise is a large part of life. They will have more to offer, and they will gain more satisfaction from executing their craft well.

Competence: Entrance into the "Adult Club"

Teaching your children competence helps them move toward adulthood. In a way, adults form an exclusive club—it's not open to all who want to join. The club has requirements for membership.

The first requirement is to be competent in some area. Children need to have a function or service to offer to the adult club. When they are young, your children's job is simply to grow up; it is not to contribute to the betterment of grown-ups. Learning to master some ability, however, is part of the process of bringing children into the adult world. Mastery says, "I can and will make a contribution," whether it be teaching, plumbing, surgery, or business. "Do you see a man skilled in his work? He will serve before kings; he will not serve before obscure men" (Proverbs 22:29).

The second requirement is to become equal and mutual with adults. Children have moms and dads to show them how to tie shoes, to help them get a driver's license, and to be a safety net when they fail. Grown-ups must do these things for themselves with no safety net. A child's need for a parent shifts from his human parents to God himself, who wants to be his only parent. As Jesus taught, "And do not call anyone on earth 'father,' for you have one Father, and he is in heaven" (Matthew 23:9). Competent people show themselves to be brothers and sisters to other adults, with God as their parent.

The third requirement is relational. Adults connect on both a bonding level and a task level. Developing some skill or expertise helps your child relate in both ways to other adults. They share the mutual task of work. The question, "So what do you do?" should be met by something meaningful besides, "I am a nice person."

Before I was married, I attended a singles retreat with other people in their mid-twenties to early thirties. Part of the process of getting to know each other was introducing what we were doing in life. Some people were in a trade, others were in business, still others were in grad school.

When the conversation turned to Dave, a handsome man in his early thirties, he started talking about his scholastic and sports achievements in high school, where he had excelled. A friend of his who knew him well enough to kid him in public finally said, "So, nothing to speak of after that?"

Although I would have fallen off my chair in embarrassment, Dave chuckled and said, "I have so much potential, it's hard to find the right niche."

Dave was a genuinely nice guy. But it was hard to relate to him in the adult club. Because he had a history of stops, starts, and turns in his career, he didn't have much of depth to talk about.

Your child's ability to master some gift or talent is also an important source of a realistic self-image and confidence. As she "owns" some interest and grows in it, she is able to experience life less as a helpless, dependent infant and more as a grownup: "the desire accomplished is sweet to the soul" (Proverbs 13:19 KJV). Growing up has its own particular sweetness. You can stay up all night working, and no one will ground you!

Love and Approval Are Different

Work and mastery are related to success, achievement, and performance. Because of this relationship, some parents may be concerned about things like performance anxiety and conditional love based on achievement. They don't want their kid to work hard to be loved. There are too many stories of people who worked hard to earn love, and they lived as miserable successes. But these problems aren't caused by learning competence and mastery. These involve a different need in life.

Your child should not have her love needs tied to her performance. She should be secure in her relationship to you with no strings attached. This is the essence of grace—love that one doesn't deserve. You are "for" your child, no matter how good, bad, industrious, or lazy she is. Love and approval are two different things.

You need to help your child gain an approval that is tied to performance—the approval of earning adult status in the world. By her competence and skill she is qualifying to enter adult realms. She has paid her dues, done her homework, and learned her craft. She earns respect, equality, opportunities, chances that others don't get, a good position and paycheck, among other good things. As the Bible teaches, "Do your best to present yourself to God as one approved, a workman who does not need to be ashamed" (2 Timothy 2:15).

This is a good and fair thing. We do no favors to anyone by removing the rewards of hard work or by giving those rewards to the underperforming. Remember, keep love and approval separate. As a parent, you tell her, "I love you with no strings attached. However, I don't approve of how you are handling the jobs we are giving you."

Work Is Good, Important, and Expected

Developing your child's competency first involves helping him create a "pro-work" attitude. You need to provide an environment in which he can internalize the reality that work is good, important, and expected. He needs to make friends with work early in life and understand that it is just as much a part of life as attachment, friends, and fun.

You already have some help from God on this end. From the womb, children are involved in some tasks. The infant playing with her toes is hard at work already, in the task of learning dexterity, delegated to her during this period of life. Your job is to help structure, focus, and deepen her involvement in work. When you observe the task energy in your children going more toward learning skateboard tricks than toward doing homework, you need to intervene and help point this energy in the right direction.

Work and Skill Are Part of Life

A high percentage of my physician friends seem to come from physician parents. I don't know if statistics bear this out, but other doctor friends of mine have said the same. I have asked several of my friends about why they became doctors. They have all said the same thing: dinner conversation. Dad or Mom or both would talk about their work, and the kids were fascinated. They heard stories about bloody surgeries, investigative victories of tricky diagnoses, and people's gratitude for their healing. Sounds as good as a TV drama. The children grew up with parents who loved their work, were really good at it, helped people, and received a great deal of satisfaction from it.

Not many parents are cardiac surgeons, but most parents do something worthwhile. Your child needs to see you involved in your work and bringing the interesting part of it to the family conversation. Your child tends to see work as something that takes you away from her, and that is a bad thing. Model interest in, involvement in, even frustration with your job. Let her see you love her, but you have a work life, too. Take her to your job site. Do a show-and-tell about your career at her classroom. She needs to internalize an emotional picture of someone who is mastering some niche in life.

Values

Your work is, at some level, tied into your values. You have chosen a certain path and specialty because of what you believe is important in life. Educators believe in the value of schooling. Business people believe in a product or service. Your values integrate your work into your life, mission, and meaning. Talk to your child about why you do what you do and why you think it's important. She needs to see how work is part of the big picture of life.

Habits

Modeling also involves not only your involvement in work, but your work ethic and habits. If you want a child who is on time, finishes tasks, and follows instructions, be that person. Walk your talk. Your child listens harder to what you do than what you say. Provide a picture of an industrious person who plays well, relates well, and works well.

Expect the same from your child. Finishing an assigned task, doing it thoroughly, and completing it *with minimum parental supervision* are good work habits. The more you have to stand over her shoulder to get her to clean the tub, the more you are helping her see work as something she doesn't have to own. Set consequences for work not completed without supervision, and praise staying on task.

Attitudes

Grumbling is a part of work life ever since the Fall, when Adam and Eve's work changed from being joyful to "painful toil" (Genesis 3:17). You can't ask a child to whistle while he works. But you can require him to keep his protests respectful. "Aw, Mom, I don't feel like mowing the lawn" is acceptable, as long as he is starting up the lawnmower at the time.

Your child's attitude also needs to involve appreciating the value of what he's doing. Your own work attitudes, praise for his work, and valuing what he does for the family will help him develop this. Internalization helps this move from being dependent on your praise to an inner sense of satisfaction in a job well done.

Normalization

In addition, normalize work for your child. Let her know that you expect her to work most of her life. Work is an integral part of life. The parent who lives for the weekend and for vacations is helping a child internalize the view that work is to be tolerated, not undertaken wholeheartedly.

Delegation

Children should be shouldering age-appropriate tasks. At the proper time, give them jobs they can do in the home. This might mean cleaning up, putting clothes in the hamper, sweeping, and doing kitchen duties. As they grow, these tasks can also grow in complexity and difficulty. For example, sweeping the porch may develop into doing yard work. Or washing dishes may evolve into planning and preparing meals. Let them know that a family is a team, and the team works together. Provide consequences when one member doesn't pull her weight.

Work and Money

We don't believe in paying a child for chores. Family members should be expected to contribute to a smooth-running family home. You don't want to create a kid who feels entitled to stick his hand out for a tip when you ask him to help you rake leaves. This sets him up for lots of problems in his career path. Instead, help your child develop the attitude Jesus taught: "So you also, when you have done everything you were told to do, should say, 'We are unworthy servants; we have only done our duty'" (Luke 17:10).

We suggest, instead, that on a regular basis you give your children some money not tied to chores. This money is theirs for certain expenditures like toys, snacks, or clothing. Don't buy those items anymore for the child; when the money is gone, the items don't arrive in the home. Various financial systems can help you determine how much of an allowance to give children at what ages. You can find them in bookstores that carry family products.

This amount needs to include money for tithing and savings, with the remainder left for spending. Give your children the gross amount, then have them put the tithe and savings amounts in a separate place. This helps them to experience taking home an after-tax paycheck so they get used to the idea that what you earn isn't what you can spend. Many adults still haven't put that one together!

Skill

In work, it's not enough to show up and participate. Results do matter. Help your child learn the importance of skill and achievement. Many parents fear challenging their kid to certain standards of performance, and you do have to be careful about demanding too much. However, a parent's fear is often based on her inability to separate love and approval, as we mentioned before. A well-loved, secure child can be challenged to do better based on both the carrot and the stick, as long as the love is constant.

Being afraid to challenge your child to higher skill levels can result in a caring, loving, nice, "slacker" kid. This child is good at heart, but has very little capacity or desire to work, create, or solve problems. Think about what the future holds for him when he leaves home, and get him working on something now.

When I was in college, one of my summer jobs was working at an ice-cream truck manufacturing plant. I helped insulate the inside of truck bodies. One day everyone in my crew was absent from work but me, so I was in charge of insulation. I worked hard for several hours and thought I was doing a good job. But after I finished my first truck, the plant manager took one look at it and ripped out my work. I had to start all over again. We talked about what I couldn't do (almost everything), and the next truck went a lot better. Skill is more than showing up with good intentions and effort. It also means doing something well.

Creativity and Problem Solving

The heart of work is creating good things and solving problems. Either you're putting together a marketing plan to blow the socks off the competition, or you're finding a way to save lots of overhead. Getting your child involved in tasks is inviting him to these fundamental aspects of work. Use his schoolwork, chores, and outside jobs to help him learn creativity and problem solving.

Washing dishes involves more than rinsing out cereal bowls. Have your child figure out how to take a frying pan with burnt grease on it and, using soap, water, a bristle brush, time, and elbow grease, get it shiny again. Get her to set up a system of homework times that she can and will adhere to. Help her think beyond just doing exactly what you ask and no more.

Evaluation

It helps kids to be graded on their performance. They need to experience success and failure. Being graded helps them to monitor their ways and make necessary corrections. It reinforces responsibility and punishes slothfulness. God will evaluate us all someday on how we lived our lives: "For we must all appear before the judgment seat of Christ, that each one may receive what is due him for the things done while in the body, whether good or bad" (2 Corinthians 5:10).

We don't believe in eliminating failure from a child's experience. This doesn't ready him for a world that has a lot to do with failure. Teach him to fail well and learn from the failure.

Competition

Mastering tasks often involves some conflict with and comparison to other children. The kid at the next desk may be a faster reader. One sibling may be better at sports than another. In competition, one strives for mastery in order to defeat an adversary: "Do you not know that those who run in a race all run, but only one receives the prize? Run in such a way that you may win" (1 Corinthians 9:24 NASB).

Competing is by nature a good thing, as it helps children adapt to realities such as team cooperation, others' competition, and goal motivations. Help your children know how to compete well. However, competition should not be a big deal in the early years. It should gradually increase as a child's maturity to handle it increases

Be aware of the competitive bind that you can sometimes get into with your kids. Help them know how to accept loss. In addition, help them to preserve their relationship with competitors. NBA players are serious opponents on the court, defending their territories. But between games, many opposing teammates are good friends. They value relationship above competition.

Fears of Success and Failure

Your child will most likely struggle with fears of both doing well and of failing in life. These two different struggles have much to do with his relationship with you as the parent.

Children fear success for various reasons. Some kids don't perform up to their potential because they are afraid a parent will envy their success and punish them for making the parent look inferior. Others fear ridicule from peers. Still others are afraid that they will then be expected to handle even more, so they underperform. Some are reacting to a parent who they feel is pushing them too hard or is living through their achievements. If your child is struggling in this regard, get him to open up about his fears. Reassure him of your love and your support for his successes.

Having anxiety about failure is a good thing at a certain level. Anxiety can motivate, bring focus, and help us follow through well on tasks. However, failure anxiety that lowers achievement and paralyzes success is a problem. Some kids get so scared during school tests that they can't finish, or they suffer from brain fade. Some can't perform well in sports, fearing that they may make mistakes.

Failure anxiety may have to do with one of several things. Sometimes this anxiety means a child is afraid you will withdraw love from him or that he will incur your wrath. Sometimes he sees himself as an all-bad person, too imperfect to be loved. If these are factors, take steps to repair this fear so that he can return to normal levels of anxiety. Get him to talk about what he is scared of. Reassure him of your unconditional love, or that you won't become angry, or that you also make mistakes. Give him time and opportunities to grow in this area.

Developing Talents and Gifts

Not only do you want to help your children learn how to integrate work into their lives, you also want to help them with the specific interests, talents, gifts, and aptitudes God put into them in potential form. Parenting involves helping your children explore, discover, and develop those capacities that they will later enjoy and excel in.

Discovering Talents

Within your child's soul are certain aptitudes waiting to emerge and bloom into talents and gifts. God has done his job, and your job is to invite your child to engage in various experiences so that you and she can figure out what she values, excels in, and loves doing.

My own father, who is now retired, is highly skilled in radio electronics. He has been in radio since he was a child. He did radio work in the U.S. Navy in World War II. He raised four kids on what he earned with his expertise. If you were in eastern North Carolina and your business had radio problems no one else could fix, you called Jack Townsend.

My father invited me to his shop, showed me what he did, and let me do some part-time work. Dad helped me try out electronics to see if it was something at which I'd be competent. It wasn't. He and I both discovered that I had little talent or interest in radio or technical fields.

Sometime in junior high, however, we were talking about jobs, and he said, "You know, you're good with people. Why don't you think about becoming an attorney?" I didn't do much with the attorney part (except that I have a good collection of lawyer jokes), but his casual statement resonated inside me.

Through college, work, and grad school, the helping professions attracted me. I went in many directions to get there, involving myself in parachurch organizations, the pastorate, the mission field, and group home settings, and I finally ended up in counseling.

In his involved but hands-off way, Dad helped me find what I love to do. Although I'm not a hands-on technical person, I love the technical aspects of my profession: the details of theology and psychological research. But I am glad the world has been spared from my involvement in Dad's kind of technical realms.

From an early age, children will benefit from what is called a stimulus-rich environment: lots of different activities to engage in at appropriate developmental levels. Before school age, have interactive toys and art supplies that will help children imagine and create. As they get older, expose them not only to school, but to sports, the arts, the sciences, church involvement, and helping others. *These play tasks are the beginnings of what will ultimately become work tasks.* Your child is working by playing. Make new, healthy extracurricular structures a norm in the family. This is a time of invitation and encouragement.

A family I know with three daughters has a pattern of each child's trying one different sport, activity, or art form every year. As they have gotten older, the kids have centered on things they really like. But by the time they were in junior high, they had experienced soccer, basketball, baseball, swimming, golf, tennis, chess, ballet, piano, singing, charity work, and more. It is no wonder that these three girls are also responsible baby-sitters with solid work habits and in high demand in the neighborhood and the community.

Development

Invite your children to discover their interests. And when they have latched onto some interest and invested time and energy in it, challenge them to develop their talent. Then they will be engaging in activities they enjoy and do well and with which they may have lifelong involvement. Help them to deepen their involvement and mastery.

Interest alone will not cause your children to develop competency in their chosen area. By and large, kids don't have the internalized structure to work on a specific task. They need a parent's structure to help schedule, stick with, and improve in the area they have chosen, until structure has become a part of them.

Some parents like to be guided by their child's interest level. They feel that if their child gets bored with some activity, that's a sign that he needs to move to something else. This has merit in the early years. For example, a preschooler may need to switch from artwork to singing to stories, as he cannot concentrate on anything for very long. However, kids also have a need to learn discipline, commitment, and task completion as they grow older. It is a rare child who will say, "I'm tired of recess. May I please have some multiplication drills?"

Here is where you need to act as a coach. Help your child see that commitment, investment, practice, and energy all translate to expertise in a task or talent. Give them the long-term experience. Don't let them quit team sports or other activities and lessons before the end of the season, or even a few seasons, unless there is a serious problem. For example, a child whose behavior is so disruptive that his conduct ruins the entire team's practices might need to be pulled out. However, this should not be rewarded by time at home hanging out and watching TV. The time that would have been spent on the team needs to be spent doing chores, helping out at church, or being involved in another team sport in which the child's behavior is not as negative. But a child who simply whines that he is tired of the sport should be told, "I know, honey. It's hard to stick to things you've committed to. But you signed up for this sport, and you need to finish it out for yourself and for the team."

The Basics

All the while that you are guiding your child in learning mastery in specialty areas, she should also be gaining competency in the universal areas of life that all adults need—areas such as academics, problem solving, social skills, language, hygiene and health, and home maintenance. Keep your child balanced in her grasp and mastery of what life and work are about. If she is gifted in some area, you have a duty to provide extra resources to develop the talent. However, don't neglect her life-skill growth. We have all heard stories of the child prodigy who could manage neither her career nor her love life when she grew up.

The Parent as Background

Understand your role in helping your child develop mastery. You are in the background, providing a structure for her to experience growth. Keep your own achievement and competence needs separate from hers.

- Don't be a stage parent, overinvolved in your child's stardom because of your own needs.
- Don't control the rate of accomplishment. Stay tuned to experts who can help you know what to anticipate in your child.
- Don't center your child's life around her gift. Make sure she has lots of other good things and friends. Keep a balanced life. She needs a place to be a "regular kid."
- Don't idealize your child. She is still dealing with self-centeredness, entitlement, dishonesty, and irresponsibility. Give her good reality checks. Keep giving her grace and truth through these.

It is a great calling to help your child find and grow in competence in both special areas and life's tasks. Keep picturing her as a future adult in whom you are investing time to help her prepare for entering the adult world.

Ages and Stages

Kids are always working on something. They have God-given blueprints geared toward mastering life. The following table provides some general guidelines to help you focus on which age-appropriate tasks they can be about:

Infancy	Learning basic survival skills
	Developing physically
	Crawling
	Distinguishing colors, faces, etc.
	Learning daytime and nighttime rhythms
	Working out communication with mother
Toddlerhood	Learning home schedule and rules
	Learning to speak and to interact socially
	Mastering eating with the proper utensils and going to the toilet
	Learning about life by playing
Childhood	Mastering school habits such as verbal and math skills, studying, and paying attention in class
	Playing sports and engaging in the arts
	Doing chores at home
	Cooperating with team members and competing against other teams
Adolescence	Mastering scholastic expertise and interest areas, such as science, humanities, or social studies
	Exploring talents and gifts
	Working at outside jobs
College	Being able to live on one's own
	Progressing toward mastery based on values, interests, and abilities

Creating a Workaholic?

Some parents fear that modeling, inviting, and challenging children to work will result in an adult who is addicted to his job and has no other life. Indeed, there are many workaholics out there. However, a healthily involved parent doesn't cause this. Most of the time, deficits in other character areas cause the child to fill up some vacuum with work. If attachment, responsibility, and reality are all in their proper perspective in his character development, work capacities find their own place inside the child.

Workaholics often find respite from their fears of closeness, inability to make attachments, problems in setting limits with others, and anxieties about failure. As these are resolved, work tends to become less important and more fulfilling for the adult. Work is a great servant and a poor master.

Mastery of work is one of the most rewarding aspects of child rearing for the parent because it provides an opportunity to see measurable growth.

But a working child isn't necessarily a moral child. In the next chapter we will take a look at the important character task of conscience development.

——— Eight ———

Making a Conscience

Morality

Pretend for a moment that you are spying on a group of kids who are considering doing something "against the rules," something all of them know they shouldn't do. In their discussion they give the following reasons for not doing it:

"I'm not going to do that. My mom would kill me."

"I'm not, either. I would feel really bad. I don't even think I'd enjoy it."

"No way am I going to, either. We might get caught."

"I don't think it's a good idea at all. We might get hurt."

"Me, neither. It's wrong."

"I really don't want to. I think it would make my parents sad."

As you hear these kids discuss the potential consequences of their upcoming choice, which child would you like to be yours? All of them have decided not to break the rules, but for different reasons. Some are keeping the rule because of fear of punishment, getting caught, or getting in trouble with a parent. Others have internal reasons, such as how he might feel or how he would like to keep the rules. Another one is concerned about the effect of his behavior on his parents. Is there a difference? Are all of these good reasons? Does it matter?

These children were considering an action and whether or not they were going to choose to do it. Who was guiding the children through the decision-making process? Their parents were not there—or were they?

We would contend that, to some degree, the parents were there. Not physically, of course, but the "internal parent" who helps the child to develop moral awareness and decision making was there. God has wired us to internalize our parents' guidance, values, and correction so that these things become part of us and guide us through life. As Proverbs says, "Train a child in the way he should go, and when he is old he will not turn from it" (22:6). So, to some degree, a parent is always "in the room" with a child in that the parent's training stays with a child and is part of his internal guidance system, or conscience.

How is a child's conscience developed? Can it be injured? Can it be healed? Are there better ways to develop a conscience than others? What should you focus on as you think about moral development in your children? What morals are important?

We will look at these issues in this chapter on conscience and morals.

What Is a Conscience?

Have you ever thought about what a conscience is? Most people probably haven't. I heard one person define *conscience* as "that part of you that tells you you've done something wrong and makes you feel bad about it." Many people accept this definition. We need to know right from wrong and to have a response inside of us when we violate a standard.

But beyond this, defining *conscience* is complicated. Biblical theologians differ widely on the topic. So do psychologists. They argue, for example, about whether the conscience is a distinct part of a person or not. Christian theologians argue whether it is God-given or a God-replacement. Others argue about how it should function. For instance, have you ever thought about where the right or wrong in someone's conscience comes from? Or what you are to feel when that standard is violated? Should you feel bad? How bad? For how long? Should you feel guilty? Is the standard automatically right? Can you have a "wrong standard" in your conscience? How would you know?

The subject of conscience brings up these kinds of problems. But these are more than technical questions for theologians and psychologists. They are very important questions for a parent to ask. God has granted you the responsibility for developing your child's sense of moral awareness, which includes the following:

- An awareness of right and wrong
- The morals that will guide your child
- An internal ability to weigh moral decisions
- An ability to self-correct
- A proper internal response to violating a standard
- A desire to do right

If you send your child into adulthood with the above list, you will have done well. Let's look at how you can develop your child's moral awareness, what gets in the way, and what will help.

Three Big Things Worth Worrying About

In our experience, all parents have a problem. We parents worry a lot. But the problem is not *that* we worry, it's *what* we worry about. It is good for us to worry, but we have to worry about the right things. Some of us worry too much about the wrong things and not enough about the really important things.

There are three things we want you to examine continually throughout the course of your children's growing up years, things that have to be monitored and changed continually. These three things are:

- That they develop a conscience
- The tone of the conscience
- The content and quality of the conscience

That They Develop a Conscience

The overall guiding principles of the moral development of children are

- Developing a moral awareness of right and wrong
- Developing an inclination to do what is right
- Experiencing internal consequences if they do wrong.

Because they are created in the image of God, children are born with an internal moral orientation, but it has to be shaped. You are an external conscience for your children, and through experience, this external conscience becomes internal. So your first task is to let your children know right from wrong. Set limits for your children—things you allow and things you don't. Setting limits can start very early in life, sometime around the end of the first year and into toddlerhood. Around this time, they need to bump into limits and learn that they will suffer something if they do not respect your no.

Your no is a good thing. It will guard your child's life for the rest of her days. The content will change over the years. Eventually she will be able to go out into the street, for example. But the no the toddler receives for crawling too far is the same no that she hears when she contemplates cheating on her spouse. "Don't crawl out of the yard" changes into "Don't cheat on your spouse." The function is the same; the content is different. What is important is that the child is learning the value of no early in life and learning to respect it.

We will talk about specific content later. But for now, remember that your child needs limits. He needs to find out that he is not in control of the universe, and ultimately his conscience will tell him this. It will help remind him that he is subject to a higher moral order. For now, though, that order is you. And if you do not set limits, then your child will be without moral order later, which will destroy his life. As Proverbs 5:23 warns us, "He will die for lack of discipline, led astray by his own great folly."

At the same time, don't be too rigid. Every moral stage of life must have freedom. Adam and Eve only had one rule! Don't have so many nos that your limits have no meaning. If everything is a no, then "no" has no meaning. Give your children moral freedom from crawling and exploring to making mistakes as they learn. But set limits somewhere, especially in areas of danger, which is one of the guidelines underlying morality even at the highest stages.

The idea of "that they have a conscience" means that you are not allowing your children to get away with things that they should not get away with, at whatever stage. Remember that a rule without enforcement teaches children that they are above the law and that morals are just suggestions. If you are flimsy about being able to discipline and follow through, get help. It will save the life of your child. "He who spares the rod hates his son, but he who loves him is careful to discipline him" (Proverbs 13:24).

So, the first thing to worry about is whether you have the ability to have limits, to set them, and to follow through with them. Remember what we said earlier: *what was once outside becomes inside.* If you have limits on the outside for your child and you follow through with them, your child will internalize them. If you don't, she won't have any either. Do not look at discipline as a small thing, something that you can postpone "because it feels so mean." The reality is that if you don't discipline, or if one parent leaves it up to the other, then there will be the absence of a moral order within your child. You must make sure that your children have a conscience.

The Tone of the Conscience

The second thing you must worry about, which is just as important as the first, is the tone of the conscience. An angry conscience cannot be used by your child. It becomes his adversary. It's like an internal machine gun waiting to murder his spirit any time he makes a mistake.

According to the Bible, there are two ways of living. One is "under the law," and the other is "under grace." The law is a system of rules we must obey or we incur wrath, condemnation, and loss of love. We get attacked as "bad," and we end up alienated. Then we focus on performance to regain love and not feel so bad. The tone of the law is:

- Angry
- Adversarial
- Harsh
- Condemning
- Guilt-producing

- Alienating
- Performance-motivating to gain love

The tone of grace is the opposite. While grace agrees with the content of the law—that is, that rules are good—it has a different orientation. Grace does not possess wrath, anger, condemnation, alienating guilt, loss of relationship, or the like. As we said earlier, grace is *for* the child, not *against* him. So the tone of grace is:

- Loving
- Nurturing
- On the same team as the child
- Forgiving
- Connecting
- Empowering
- Performance-motivating from a loved position

Why do we include this as one of the three things to worry about? Because the tone of your child's conscience will determine, to some degree, whether your child will follow it. You can build morals within a child, but if the tone of their conscience is of the law, they ultimately will not follow it or they will break their necks trying to satisfy it. It is one of the basic promises of the Bible. According to Paul's letter to the Romans, the law increases sin (5:20), and it creates wrath (4:15). And saddest of all, the law does not help anyone get better (Hebrews 7:18–19). It may lead to external conformity, but it does not affect the heart.

If you discipline a child with the emotional tone of the law, you can expect the same: an increase of the problem, anger, guilt, performance orientation, and ultimately lack of self-control.

Therefore, not only must a child "have a conscience," but also it must be his friend. It must be loving, correcting, and empowering to do the right thing. It must, as we will see, cause your child to be more concerned with others than his own guilt. In short, like the grace of God, it must be strong, but kind. It must be serious, but compassionate. It must seek the child's well-being by leading him in the direction that is good for him in the long run.

Where will he get such a conscience? Remember, "what was once outside becomes inside."

The Content and Quality of the Conscience

Now that you have decided to give your child a moral awareness and that it should be a nice enforcer, what are the laws of the land? On what are you going to focus? What kind of content is going to be written on the heart of your child?

Certainly, the content is going to change with the age of the child. For a toddler, it may be "Don't touch the stove." For a teenager, it may be "If you don't cook dinner, you won't go to the movies." Very different content. So don't get too caught up in making small things absolutes. But here are a few things to keep in mind.

First, the final outcome of moral training is love. As Jesus said, the entire book of God's law could be summed up in the two laws, "Love God, and love your neighbor as yourself" (see Matthew 22:37–39). Any moral training must have relationship as its underlying reason for existence. If one departs from the moral training, someone gets hurt. Someone suffers.

Therefore, as soon as possible you should focus on the "whys" of what you are doing. Not "Don't call your sister stupid. That's a sin," but "Don't call your sister stupid. That hurts her feelings. Do you like it when someone calls you names?" The latter is more relational.

When Jesus commanded us to love others as ourselves, he was not teaching "self-love." He was teaching about the deep connection of empathy. As a result of our actions, we identify with how the other person feels. We care about their pain as if it were our own. Teach your children that their behavior affects others.

There is a reason that children need to be on time for dinner. It is not because there is something inherently holy about eating at seven o'clock, but because others would have to wait for them if they are late. So, to a late child we might say, "Since we don't want others to suffer, we will go ahead and eat without you so your tardiness only affects you and not other people." That is moral.

A teenage boy should hear that it grieves God for him to have premarital sex, to have him love his own impulses more than God. He is cheating on God. That hurts God. Also, is he considering what he is doing to the young woman? To her future husband? How does he feel about taking something so precious from her and leaving her with the memory of having given herself away for nothing permanent? He is hurting her. And how about himself? Does he realize that he is hurting himself? Does he know that he is splitting his personality by giving himself physically to someone to whom he is not giving the rest of himself? A lack of holiness is inevitably self-destructive in some way.

The Bible always teaches morality in the bigger context of hurting and rejecting God, hurting and splitting oneself, and hurting others. Notice all three in 1 Thessalonians 4:3–8:

> It is God's will that you should be sanctified: that you should avoid sexual immorality; that each of you should learn to control his own body in a way that is holy and honorable, not in passionate lust like the heathen, who do not know God; and that in this matter no one should wrong his brother or take advantage of him. The Lord will punish men for all such sins, as we have already told you and warned you. For God did not call us to be impure, but to live a holy life. Therefore, he who rejects this instruction does not reject man but God, who gives you his Holy Spirit.

As children get older and can understand, your need is to focus on the relationship as underlying morality. When they are very young, this is not possible. But soon in childhood, they can discover that it hurts others to be mean.

Second, morals are to protect our lives and to ensure a good life. Morals are not killjoys. They are the principles that undergird success in life. As God said, when your child asks, "Why do we have to keep all these rules?" let them know that it is so

life will go better for them. Rules will help them. It will make
them successful. Listen to the way God puts it:

> In the future, when your son asks you, "What is the mean-
> ing of the stipulations, decrees and laws the LORD our God
> has commanded you?" tell him: "We were slaves of Pharaoh
> in Egypt, but the LORD brought us out of Egypt with a
> mighty hand. Before our eyes the LORD sent miraculous
> signs and wonders—great and terrible—upon Egypt and
> Pharaoh and his whole household. But he brought us out
> from there to bring us in and give us the land that he
> promised on oath to our forefathers. The LORD commanded
> us to obey all these decrees and to fear the LORD our God,
> so that we might always prosper and be kept alive, as is
> the case today. And if we are careful to obey all this law
> before the LORD our God, as he has commanded us, that
> will be our righteousness (Deuteronomy 6:20–25).

Living morally leads to a successful life: successful relationships, successful careers, and the successful use of one's talents.
Morality is not about enforcing a bunch of rules for no reason.
Take heed of the way God sees the issue, and do not become a
"religious" moralist. Do not be more interested in rules, and in
goodness versus badness, than in love and reality. Your children
will reject moralism, and it will not serve them well. But reality
will serve them well.

When they are young, your children won't understand this,
but you can teach them by letting them suffer reality consequences when they break a rule. Reality consequences, instead
of anger, guilt, and alienation, teach your children early that
God's laws are there for a reason. "If I do wrong, I suffer," the
child learns. Even though the suffering may be small to you, such
as grounding, it is large to him. This suffering as a consequence
teaches a blueprint for life.

As they get older, you can teach your children the principle
of wisdom. Wisdom teaches that there are positive and negative reasons for any moral law. The positive one is that life works

best when you live it as it was designed. Diligence makes people successful. Courage takes us to new heights. The negative reason is that life does not work when you don't live it as it was designed. Lying destroys relationships. Drugs fry your brain and ruin your life. Sleeping around can kill you. Cheating lands you in jail.

The emphasis here is on reality. You don't need to use punitive anger, guilt, or alienation to make your child obey you. Reality successes feel good, and reality consequences don't. Reality successes like working hard and selling enough cookies to win the ski trip feel good; reality consequences like missing the fishing outing because homework was not done do not feel good. Your job is to make those consequences a reality early for your children, and then gradually turn them into principles they can understand. The role of the conscience is not to produce guilt. The role of the conscience is to produce an awareness of right and wrong related to love and the reality of God's laws. It is much better for your children to be able to observe themselves, evaluate their behavior, and change than for them to beat themselves up for things they think, feel, or do.

So, the content of the conscience will change as your child grows. But it should always be moving toward protecting love with God and others as well as aligning oneself with the reality of God's created order. Focus on relationship more than petty rules. Focus on reality issues and reality consequences more than petty rules. Then you will have a child who is headed for a life of producing and protecting love as well as being able to function in reality.

The Process

As we said earlier, the moral functioning of a child is developmental, just as was God's revelation to humankind. For instance, God gave the law to Moses and the children of Israel, and then he fulfilled it with the principle of love and internal motivation through Jesus. This is a good metaphor for the development of a child.

In the early stages, children understand the law. A child's early sense of morality is based on her own pain and external consequences. It goes something like this: "I feel bad, I must have been bad." This is why infants with a lot of uncomforted pain and aloneness, such as being left alone crying and hungry too often, grow up with critical consciences. The early states of "bad feeling" created a "bad me" structure. Love and care transform a sense of pain or badness in a small child.

Soon after infancy, a child's sense of morality changes to "I got spanked or scolded; therefore I was bad." Morality is based on "what I get in trouble for." If there is some external bad happening, a child thinks that it has moral meaning. They think, for example, that they did something bad if their parents divorce: "My parents got a divorce because I am bad."

This is an important time for parents. Giving consequences begins to form their children's conscience and helps with some of the irrational thinking involved in the 'bad happening=I'm bad' morality. The children learn right from wrong based on what happens when they do *a* or *b*. They are also getting a bigger picture of when "Mommy or Daddy is pleased, or not." This slowly translates into "My conscience is pleased, or not."

As children mature and can understand higher forms of language, they begin to get their first view of real morality. They begin to understand right from wrong on a conceptual level. This continues through adolescence, when they begin to understand it on a principle level.

The progression goes something like this:

1. Bad Feeling States = Bad, Good Feeling States = Good
2. Good Results or Consequences =Good, Bad Results or Consequences = Bad
3. Rules and External Authority Tell Me What Good and Bad Are, and Consequences Prove That
4. Understand Principles and Move to Internal Consequences

Your Own Ten Commandments

Children are building values and morality in the context of relationship. God planned it this way. Your laws, as you teach them and as you live them, are being written on their hearts. These become part of their consciences, through identification, imitation, modeling, and experience.

Identification is the process by which children take in their parents at a very unconscious level. Children form their personalities from a parent. You may be amazed to see your son or daughter using the same expressions or gestures as you or your spouse. In the same way, they are identifying with you as a moral agent. They unconsciously "take you in." They will feel your attitudes toward things, and those attitudes will likely become part of them.

Imitation is more active. Children will imitate your behavior to learn how to behave. They will mimic you to learn how to talk, gesture, or deal with situations. For example, you may hear a young child disciplining her dolly in the same way you discipline her. I laughed the other day as John's five-year-old son, Bennie, mimicked my disciplining of my German shepherd. Bennie pointed his finger at Bonnie, who is as big as he is, and forcefully said, "No!" He was getting it.

Modeling is the taking on of roles and abilities, such as the role of being male or female, and the ability of how to treat people. Children model your compassion, forgiveness, and sacrifice, and they also model your harshness, anger, and self-centeredness. What you show your children is what they become. Children look to you, and especially a same-sex parent, to answer the question "How do I do this?" All the time you are showing them how to be moral people. If you say, "Lying is wrong," and then, when the phone rings, you ask them to say to the caller, "Tell her I'm not here," you model that lying is okay. When you tell your daughter to be nice to her little brother and then you yell at him, you are saying one thing and modeling another.

Jesus showed us how to love; he is not afraid of being looked at as a model. The apostle John tells us, "Whoever claims to live in him must walk as Jesus did" (1 John 2:6). As the apostle Paul played the role of "parent" to other believers, he took on his role as model unreservedly: "Even though you have ten thousand guardians in Christ, you do not have many fathers, for in Christ Jesus I became your father through the gospel. Therefore I urge you to imitate me" (1 Corinthians 4:15–16). Grasp the same courage and fervor they did in your role as model to your children. As the old saying goes, "the apple does not fall far from the tree." Your children will imitate you.

And then they will also *experience* you directly. I once explained to a group of adults how the family is a spiritual system. Just as God gave his family (the children of Israel) a set of commandments to follow, parents give their family their own set. It is given not only in stone, but with experience. I asked the group members to write the relational theology they learned from experience with their parents. Here were some examples:

- Thou shalt not speak the truth about certain issues. It will make your father angry.
- Thou shalt not display sadness. It angers your mother.
- Thou shalt not make a mistake, ever. You should already know how to do it before you are told.
- Thou shalt be able to guess the mood of your father and not disturb him.
- Thou shalt not want to be independent. It is an abomination.

You get the idea. None of these families would put these commandments on the wall of the kitchen in embroidery to be memorized. But they were memorized because they were experienced by the children and became part of their own conscience. Later in life, when a relationship would call for direct truth, or sadness, or forgiveness, or independence, the children's conscience would not allow them to bring forth those qualities. And their adult relationships suffered. Remember, no matter what you believe, how you relate to your children is forming their conscience. Their brains are recording as rules your responses to them.

I have worked with many adults who are afraid to take risks and pursue dreams. Every time a desire emerges inside them, a strict conscience says, "What do you want that for? You don't need that." Or, "That will never work. You can't do that." Or, "You are so selfish for wanting that." They do not have internal permission to pursue their talents and dreams. They fear failure if they try. They have become prisoners to their unbiblical conscience. This is what we were referring to above when we said that the conscience can contain things that are not right. The conscience is not without error; it has to be carefully shaped.

Therefore, when your children make mistakes, show emotion, are assertive, or become sexual beings, how you respond to them will dictate how available those parts become to them later in life. React with shame, anger, or guilt, and they will repress and lose aspects of who they are. React with grace and truth, and those parts of their personalities will get structured into a conscience that allows them to use them in the right ways. You are writing your own Ten Commandments onto your children's hearts and minds with every interaction.

Another aspect of this dilemma is that two parents form a conscience. If the parents are not on the same page, a child gets a "split conscience." In other words, a child may end up with a strict part and a permissive part. If Dad is loose and Mom is strict, the child will have two parts of himself that disagree.

You may have experienced this division within yourself. You go on a spending spree and then punish yourself with guilt and a period of austerity. A few months later, you are back at it, running up bills, only to be followed by guilt when the other side of the split kicks in. Others experience that split with food, sex, or an assortment of "forbidden fruits." The permissive parent inside says, "Oh, it's okay." The person binges, and then the strict one punishes her for a while. After the punishment, the permissive, enabling one comes back to comfort her in her guilt and deprivation, and the cycle starts over again.

To the best of your abilities, compare constantly with your spouse how the two of you are doing in balancing the tone, content, and quality of being the external conscience for your children. This will go a long way toward giving them one conscience instead of two. One conscience is enough for anyone to deal with.

Some Good Values

Here are some values we believe are good to instill in your children:

- Love, honor, obedience, and the pursuit of God (seek him first in everything)
- Love and its derivatives
- Compassion, forgiveness, mercy, grace, kindness
- Truth and its derivatives
- Honesty, integrity, directness, taking moral stands, confession, respect for reality
- Humility
- Faith (acting and ordering life on things unseen)
- Faithfulness and loyalty
- Service and sacrifice (giving, offering, and sacrificing of self for others and higher values)
- Stewardship (taking God's gifts and one's possessions seriously)
- Respect (for other people and their property)
- Obedience and submission (to God, parents, law and government, and other legitimate authority)
- Self-control and self-discipline (delay of gratification)
- Courage (pushing on through fear, faith, and risk-taking)
- Sexual wholeness (purity, respect for God's creation, limits, embracing and celebrating sexuality)
- Fun (celebration and enjoyment of life and God's blessings and creation)
- Development of talents and work (congruence with pursuing the true self that God created)
- Furthering God's life to others (evangelism, missions, helping)

Refer to this list throughout the development of your child. The Bible teaches that these are the basic values that life in God is built upon. If you can construct a conscience in children around these issues, you are well on the way to giving them an internal guide for the rest of their lives, a guide that will be there when you no longer are.

In the final analysis, conscience, or whatever you want to call it, is an important aspect of parenting. But just to give a child rules falls short of a biblical view of conscience, one that is psychologically and emotionally healthy and usable. Make sure that rules are focused on love, corrected by love, and built in the context of love. If you do those things, your child will one day praise you for all the discipline along the way.

In the next chapter, we will look at the deepest morality: a child's connection to God.

Nine

Connecting to God

Worship and Spiritual Life

I (Dr. Townsend) was a teen in the late sixties. Back then, my father was concerned about not only the cultural and political shifts of the day, but also the spiritual problems he saw. He liked my friends a lot, but he thought we were all ungrounded in our faith. So he did the unthinkable: he volunteered to teach Sunday school to the teens in our church. His goal was to help those who were struggling with, had questions about, or were even hostile to religion.

My father didn't really enjoy teaching. Being shy, he saw himself as a weak teacher. And adolescents aren't the most receptive group in church. He volunteered out of his values, not his interests.

Since most of the teenagers had very little scriptural background, Dad emphasized the Bible. He wanted to make the Bible interesting, so he challenged our ideas about its being boring and irrelevant. He made us read passages in the Old Testament about bloody battles, illicit relationships, and failures, and then he would say, "Now that's as down-to-earth as anything you'll find on the newsstand."

Once he devised a simple way to memorize the Ten Commandments by using mental pictures to represent each commandment. For example, the second commandment, "You shall have no other gods before me," he called "two," representing its number. He pointed out that *two* rhymes with *shoe*. To help us remember the commandment, he drew a picture of people bowing down to a giant shoe.

We weren't very appreciative, but Dad did his duty and finished his teaching stint, thinking it was pretty much a nonevent.

In the last few years, however, I have been in contact with several Sunday school classmates from the old days who have told me how much of a difference Dad's teaching made during their turbulent, searching years. Some credit him with helping them take an interest in relating to God. His fervent desire to show them that the Bible had answers for them stuck with them. And some could still recite the Ten Commandments. He did his job of sowing faithfully, and God used it to produce a good crop (Matthew 13:8).

As a parent, you may feel a tension similar to my Dad's. You have a deep desire to foster your child's spiritual life, but you wonder where to begin. This chapter resolves this tension by dealing with two aspects—being involved and having a structure in which to operate.

Character and Spirituality

Your child's spiritual life is a fundamental part of total character development, not just the developing of moral and religious character. Remember that growing character helps your child function as an adult in the world. Children demand that life adapt to them, while mature adults adapt themselves to life. As we adapt to life as it really is and give up our attempts to change it, we grow up, and life works better for us.

If being a grown-up is adapting to reality, to grow up your child needs to order his life around the Author of reality. The Bible says, "For in him we live and move and have our being" (Acts 17:28). God has designed your child—and reality—to operate in certain ways within certain parameters. Finding and responding to God's statutes and ways becomes the key to growing up. So, in that sense, the spiritual dimension of life is the most important character capacity of all.

You may know people who are loving, hard-working, and reality-based, but who have no spiritual life or interests. They have been able to learn about reality from some of God's resources, such as good people, truth, and experience. But for some reason, they don't experience God as the source of life.

You may also know highly religious folks who know the Bible well and use God talk, but their everyday lives don't reflect what they know. For them, the center of what makes them tick is not connected to the rest of "real" life. Your job as a parent is to help your child to see his life as oriented around God's realities and to live out those realities in daily existence.

You cannot separate your child's spiritual life from the rest of his life. It was meant to be integrated into all the aspects of his relationships and tasks. Spiritual character growth involves much more than religious training; it involves helping the child experience that the *essence of existence is spiritual*.

Creating a Place for Relationship to Grow

Life begins with a relationship, and spiritual life is no exception. It begins with a relationship between your child and God. The development of a spiritual relationship is extremely important during the first few years of life. Children who learn early who God is and how he wants to be with them are more able to integrate his reality into the rest of their years.

But to have a relationship requires two willing parties. You can't force your child to develop a relationship with God. God invites, but does not force himself on you or your child: "Here I am! I stand at the door and knock. If anyone hears my voice and opens the door, I will come in and eat with him, and he with me" (Revelation 3:20).

God has arranged things so that your child has a voice in when she is ready to address him. This is a sobering reminder of your limitations as a parent. You cannot guarantee that your child will want to seek God. Ultimately, this choice is hers. As the old saying goes, "God has no grandchildren." In other words, no one is related to God by virtue of the faith of their parents. A relationship with God is only between him and the person.

Your task is to do background work for your child's encounter with God. All relationships, including one with God, have a structure to them. Creating that structure is something you can do. In other words, you can *create a context that fosters connectedness to God.* If you wish to start a garden in your backyard, you need to prepare the soil, add fertilizer, water, and sunlight, and remove weeds and pests. You have maximized the optimal conditions for plant growth in your garden. In the same way, you want to create optimal conditions for your child to meet and love God. Here are some of the ways to create this context for your child to seek and find God: "Anyone who comes to [God] must believe that he exists and that he rewards those who earnestly seek him" (Hebrews 11:6).

Seeing the Eternal in the Everyday

Your child needs to approach life as if it were eternal; this is fundamental in the quest for God. One of the advantages you have in developing your child's spiritual life is that children are open to the transcendent. Especially in the years between birth and puberty, they experience the world as a supernatural place. Powerful people (called parents) govern life with magical abilities. Airplanes fly, and microwaves create instant food. Money grows on trees. The very dependency of children lends itself to their accepting a world beyond their understanding, with rules they can't comprehend.

I asked an eight-year-old boy what his earliest memory of God was. He told me he thought it was when he was in preschool; he remembered thinking God was an invisible man who flew in the clouds. God was very good and very powerful. This picture was appropriate for the boy's age and developed over the next few years into a more cohesive image of God. A superhero became a spiritual reality for him.

Help your child see the eternal in the everyday parts of life. Your child needs to experience how you interpret circumstances from a transcendent viewpoint. This might include talking about how God can help him know the right thing to do in a struggle with a neighbor friend. Or about how God has answered his prayer. Or how he can apply what he heard at church to what is happening at school.

On another level, help your child experience that the rules in both the seen and the unseen worlds are similar. Principles such as love, faithfulness, honesty, and ownership work in both worlds; they are how God governs reality. God is not in conflict with himself. As you order your child's existence to follow these universal principles, she is aligning herself to approach God. His rules will make sense to her. For example, if you model vulnerability and truth-telling in your relationship with your child, she is more likely to be able to truly understand the Bible passage that exhorts us to speak the truth in love (Ephesians 4:15). From her experience, the jump to connecting to God is a shorter one.

Seeing God as the Source of All Good Things

In their dependent role, children work hard at needing and receiving. It is hard for them to escape the humility of being without what they need and having to ask for it. However, children need to learn that asking brings us closer to God. The Bible teaches that this humility is a blessed state: "Blessed are the poor in spirit, for theirs is the kingdom of heaven" (Matthew 5:3).

Your child needs to understand that while God wants her to follow his ways, he first wants to give her the good things she needs. God is the Source of all our needs for existence, emotionally and physically. He and his resources sustain us. Talk to your child about God's provision of love, protection, information, and hope in her life. Show her that being in relationship with God is the best way to get her needs met. As one parent told me, "We are working on helping our son learn that God is a better parent to him than we are."

Your child needs to see that *you* are a better parent to him by virtue of being connected to God. As you go to the Source in prayer, worship, and study, you receive what you need to love your child better. It is sad to see children from religious families grow up dreading or hating church because it makes them feel crazy. They feel as if they have two contradictory existences: Mom and Dad do the Christian routine on Sunday, but are selfish or out of control on Monday. Much better for the children to have a parent return from church or prayer better attuned to meet their needs, one who listens better, responds appropriately, and admits wrongdoing to them. This is how they learn that good things happen when people are around God.

Life Works Better Living It God's Way

Your child needs to experience God not only as Source, but also as King. Relationship, even a divine one, always involves responsibility. God provides your child with all the good things she needs to live, but in doing so, he also requires her to order her life around his ways. How many times have you seen a grown-up who wanted the benefits of someone's love, but didn't feel a need to respond by taking ownership of her part of the relationship?

God has structured reality according to certain truths. He formalized them in the Bible so that they would be remembered accurately over the centuries. Truth exists in God's commands, laws, and principles for conducting our lives. Your children need to understand and experience these truths: "But his delight is in the law of the LORD, and on his law he meditates day and night" (Psalm 1:2)

God does not give us laws because he is a control freak. He is not interested in our obeying for obedience's sake. Rather, obedience helps us. The Bible teaches that when children ask why God has laid down all the rules and decrees that he has, you have an answer. The solution is that "the LORD commanded us to obey all these decrees and to fear the LORD our God, so that we might always prosper and be kept alive, as is the case today" (Deuteronomy 6:24). Spiritual growth and development both prosper and preserve the life of your child.

Even though she wishes to be omnipotent, a child fears making the decisions in life that adults should be making for her. She needs to know her place in the world, for in that place are security and safety: "I will walk among you and be your God, and you will be my people" (Leviticus 26:12).

Show your child that a life of obedience is a good thing. Just as house rules exist so that the family operates better, God's "house rules" of love, fairness, faithfulness, and honesty make all of life work well. In the same way, traffic lights and stop signs make our life better and safer. God doesn't want to deprive people of having fun. He wants a better life for us.

Get to know your Bible, theology, and principles as a Christian. Why do you believe the Bible is true? Why does your family go to church? Why don't you do drugs or have premarital sex? Be able to go further than "Because God says so, and he's the boss." You want your child to continually look beyond rote responses and into the deeper truths behind the commands. Talk to children about why you believe what you believe, and get them to think about the reasons for their own beliefs.

The Spiritual Disciplines and Their Purpose

Learning the truths and principles is not enough for your child's spiritual development. Parenting also involves helping her internalize the disciplines of spiritual life. Spiritual disciplines are the traditional activities people of faith have entered into for many years as a way to connect with God. Here are a few of the more central ones:

- Exposure to the Bible: hearing, reading, studying, memorizing, and meditating
- Prayer: personal communication with God, individually and in groups
- Fellowship: being in relationship with other believers, for support and reality—including church activities, family times, and small-group gatherings

The spiritual disciplines serve as a structure for your child to relate to God. They exist as a means of fostering an attachment to and service of God. They don't exist as an end in themselves.

However, they are habits that you should expect of your children, as part of what your family does.

These habits and activities should always draw your children to God's love and reality. They need to see that time and energy expended in these disciplines bring good things to them. They learn about faithfulness and openness, vulnerability and wisdom. These concepts apply to home, school, and friends.

Many people have told me about their journeys away from God when they became young adults. They were exploring and questioning everything. And many found the faith of their fathers for themselves. One thing that helped them was that they had many warm memories of living in a family with a serious, deep, and active faith. They were able to draw on memories, experiences, and even specific Bible verses as they began returning to God.

Cynthia, a friend of ours, told me that when she was working out her own adulthood, she remembered childhood times in which she would go downstairs in the middle of the night to get a glass of water. In the living room she found her reserved, detached father on his knees, praying for his family. The reality of her dad's faith never left her, even during her searching days. Now she has a great marriage, beautiful children, a good job, and a strong faith. A lot of that she credits to seeing her dad's spiritual discipline of prayer.

Sometimes, however, anxious parents will require their children to pray, read the Bible, and go to church without a real understanding of why they are doing what they're doing. They insist on the practice of the disciplines, but without integrating them into life. Their children resist all their attempts.

Roger, another friend of mine, had this experience growing up. He received much training on, and experience in, the spiritual disciplines, but without really making the ways of God a part of his life. Being around Roger is a little strange nowadays. He hates his job, argues with his parents, and has a lot of negative attitudes toward life. Then, in the middle of his protests, out of the blue he will say a Bible verse and say, "Isn't God

great?" I agree God is great, but I don't understand why griping leads to gratitude. In reality, I think Roger lives in two worlds:
the "real" world and the "spiritual" world. And he is in constant
conflict, as the two don't go together for him.

You will do well to practice the disciplines with your child.
The expression of these needs to be age-appropriate; look for one
of the many good kids' Bibles, devotional guides, and Sunday
school classes to help. Especially in the preteen years, children
want to be part of the team, and they often enjoy doing the disciplines with their family simply because they like to be involved.
But as you help them experience how these traditions help them
grow, prosper, and mature, they are able to see the reason behind
them. The disciplines are not God; they exist to serve God.

As your child grows up, his needs and interests will change.
For example, a teenager may not want to attend the church he
grew up in. He needs freedom to work out his own relationship
with God. Being in the church you chose may make it difficult
for him to own his faith. It may be a good idea, for example, to
let him find a healthy church nearby with a youth group to which
he can relate. Always keep the ends and the means separate in
issues like these. As Jesus taught, "The Sabbath was made for
man, not man for the Sabbath" (Mark 2:27).

Your Faith Matters to Your Child's Faith

More than in any other character capacity, spiritual development is "caught" more than taught. Spiritual growth involves
many conceptual understandings, so your child will internalize
more of what you *are* with God and her than what you teach.

Your own alive, defined, active, and honest faith is critical
as your child seeks to understand and attach to a vague, invisible God. Do not spare her the struggle of faith, however, to
the extent that she can developmentally understand it. Let her
see that a relationship with God, just as a relationship with anyone, takes time, has conflict, and requires work.

At some point, your child needs to take responsibility for her
own walk with God, not mimic yours. If you want a shallow or

meaningless Christianity in your child, insist that she never question your beliefs. She needs to wrestle with God for herself, and finally find God as he is, in a way that may never have worked for you.

Developmentally, this is critical, because children need to separate from their parents. If they have learned that Parents = God, they can leave God as they leave their parents. They may perceive God as someone from whom they must became independent in order to be a separate person.

Because of this, keep your child's experiences of you distinct from his experiences of God. Especially with a teenager, show him where you have failed, had doubts, or conflicted with God. Let him see you as a fellow struggler who has not plumbed all the depths and mysteries of who God is. This leaves your child room to find God anew for himself, rather than having to become his parent's child again to be religious.

A friend of mine continually read C. S. Lewis's *Chronicles of Narnia* to his son during his childhood. He was concerned about this very matter of individuation. As he explained it to me, he read Lewis because it was written in a way his son enjoyed. "I wanted him to stay with God when he was ready to leave me and my ways," he said.

Hannah, a biblical woman who suffered from infertility, understood that if God gave her a child, this child would never ultimately be hers, but God's. She prayed to God, "O LORD Almighty, if you will only look upon your servant's misery and remember me, and not forget your servant but give her a son, then I will give him to the LORD for all the days of his life" (1 Samuel 1:11). Ask God to help your child own his own faith, built on your own, but ultimately worked out by God and your child.

The Image of God Issue

The image of God issue is related to the ownership of faith issue. Some parents are concerned that their children will experience God as a composite of Dad and Mom. Basically, the thinking goes like this: Children form a mental representation of who

God is. Having nothing else to draw from, children generalize their experiences with their parents. God becomes the positives and negatives of their parents. If Dad is not emotionally there for his children, for example, God is distant. If Mom is critical of her children, God is judgmental. These parents feel a great deal of self-condemnation and pressure, for they fear that their weaknesses and foibles will cause the child to perceive God inaccurately.

We believe this thinking distorts reality. Children do internalize experiences of their parents to form an image of God; however, other important factors play a part in the development of the image of God in a child:

The child's interpretation. Memory research has shown that children interpret their experiences. Memory is not a video-tape of life. The child's own character, perspective, wishes, fears, and distortions color their memories.

Other realities. Children don't automatically assume parents equal God. As they grow, they are able to assimilate other realities, such as other people, biblical truths, and circumstances, to form an image of God.

Human and divine. Especially in the older years, children can distinguish between the attributes of people and attributes of God. They were designed with a God-shaped hole and a people-shaped hole. Maturity helps them see the difference: "God is not a man, that he should lie, nor a son of man, that he should change his mind" (Numbers 23:19).

Change and growth. A child's God-image is not static. It changes as the child matures and grows. The more experiences that reflect God, the better the child can perceive who God really is.

Give your children many experiences in which you and they draw close to God. Your children were created to seek and find him.

From Immature to Mature Dependency

There is one major difference in your child's relationship with you and with God. Your role of parent is temporary; God's is not. You are working yourself out of a job. If you are successful, your child will relate to you as an equal adult in life. So your own parenting has much to do with handing over more adult freedoms and duties to your child.

However, this is not true with your child and God. Your child was designed to be God's kid forever. He should never "leave" God and "cleave" to someone else. He is part of an eternal fatherhood-childhood covenant: "If anyone loves me, he will obey my teaching. My Father will love him, and we will come to him and make our home with him" (John 14:23).

Because of this distinction, you need to order your child's earthly child-parent relationship differently from his heavenly one. While you are helping your child to need you less, you are helping him to need God more. He is internalizing experiences with you that create capacities to function in the world without you. He is internalizing experiences with God that also create capacities to function well, but never apart from dependency on God.

You are, however, helping your child make a shift from *immature to mature dependency* on God the Father. He is a child of God, but one who is taking more responsibility in life and in how he comes to the Source of life. God is not changing; your child's needs are.

With this in mind, the table below deals with some of the age-appropriate capacities and spiritual needs of your child. Use it to help structure the ways you help your child trust and obey.

Stage	Child's Faith	Parent's Tasks
Infancy	This is a pre-faith period. Faith requires the ability to differentiate self from other, which is a task of infancy itself. This is foundational to the later experience of faith.	Help infant experience God "incarnationally." In other words, infants can't conceive of God, but they know when they are safe and loved. The infant senses the realities of dependency, goodness, and love through the relationship with

		mother or a primary caretaker.
Toddlerhood	Child begins learning dos and don'ts of God. Imitative behavior takes place as child prays and talks about God.	Make toddler part of family worship, using simple Bible stories, songs, and pictures
Childhood	Faith becomes conventional. Child learns the beliefs and doctrines of God. Not much questioning, more uncritical assimilation of vast amounts of information. Highly curious stage. Child conceptualizes God more personally. Child wants to belong.	Provide lots of teaching, both in stories and with concepts. Involve child in worship and prayer experiences. Give child sense that he belongs in spiritual family. Include child in family ministry activities.
Adolescence	The adolescent questions, challenges, and owns faith individually and personally. Has difficulties keeping God and parents separate. Needs to investigate, search, and struggle.	Provide freedom within parameters for the search. Respect dependency-independence conflict. Teach less, dialogue more. Deal with skepticism with challenge to seek. Keep church a requirement, with room for trying other youth groups.

College	Young adult deepens and consolidates faith.	Relate as spiritual sibling, not parent.
	Integrates relationship with God to other aspects of life, such as life mission, values, marriage, career.	Share struggles. Provide support for growth, deepening.
	Finds avenues of meaningful service and ministry based on faith.	

The Age of Faith?

Parents struggle with the age-old question of when to help their child make a decision of faith, to accept Christ as Savior. They wonder about the "age of accountability," the age at which a child is able to grasp the reality of Christ's death for her sins and make a profession of faith in him. They agonize over the prospect of their child making a false statement, based on compliance; then they swing over and worry that if they don't push the issue, the child might never become a believer. Many parents' most horrible nightmare is that their child will die before her time, yet after the age of accountability has occurred.

This problem can never be answered in full, as only God knows the child's heart and readiness. As well, only he knows the hour and day that our lives will be required of us (Luke 12:20). And so, the solution to this dilemma is the reality of the love of God. His love for your child is deep and abiding, and no part of him wants to play games with your child's soul: "He is patient with you, not wanting anyone to perish, but everyone to come to repentance" (2 Peter 3:9).

Two questions are worth dealing with on this topic. The first is a cognitive developmental question: *When will my child understand the gospel truths enough to make an authentic decision?* She needs to understand the following basic concepts:

- The existence and love of God
- The reality of our sinful state
- The penalty of sin
- God's provision through the death of Christ
- The requirement of accepting Christ personally

Many well-crafted materials explain these truths to children in age-appropriate ways. You might want to contact a trusted youth pastor or bookstore about them. One resource we recommend is the *NIrV Kids' Devotional Bible*.

The second question is, *how do I best create a context for my child to commit to Christ?* Do I sit down one day with her and share these truths? Do I ask her to decide? Do I tell her the facts and ask her to think about them? Do I leave it all to the church?

Your course of action depends on the nature of your child's character and her relationship with you. Ideally, if God and life go together in your home, it will make sense to the child that what you are telling her is the way to go, once she understands the truths. Everything else in her life corresponds with this. A child will often take initiative to move toward God because of this integrated home life. Or a child will grow up loving and seeking God, and one day in church or Sunday school the message will click into place in his head, and he will make a decision. Often, the context that you have been providing for years will be the most instrumental factor in the making of this decision.

However, be aware of your own emotional influence on your child, especially in the arena of his freedom to choose. Make sure the child knows his decision has nothing to do with your love and acceptance. If your child's character struggles revolve around fears of letting you down or angering you, you may want to resolve this issue first so that the child is in a position to choose. The converse is also true. A teen engaged in a fight to gain independence may reject a parent's invitation to come to God because he fears being enmeshed and controlled. Work on that issue, or let him talk to his friends at youth group, with whom those struggles aren't as intense.

Your Father in heaven wants a relationship with your child. Ask God daily how you can help and when you need to get out of the way for this process to occur in his time.

Parents are involved differently in different periods of their children's lives. This is no more evident than in the teen years, when parenting is coming to an end. We will deal with this in the next two chapters.

Part Three

Working Yourself Out of a Job

——— Ten ———

Preparing Them for Life on Their Own

"It won't be long until you're on your own, Henry, so I think you'll need to know how to manage a checking account."

This was a line I heard from my parents (with variations) a million times during adolescence. I don't think they ever took a course in child rearing, but their wisdom was apparent. They were thinking of my future. They thought I needed to know how to do a lot of different things before I left home, from managing a checking account to handling a credit card, from arranging for car insurance to planning for a career. The content of their words is not as important as their attitude toward my situation: they were seeing adolescence as a time-limited opportunity to prepare me to be on my own. I'm grateful for what they did.

A friend of mine lived in a very different situation. Although her parents never said it out loud, their actions gave a very different message from the one I received from my parents: "You are not on your own, so this is what you will do." End of conversation. The sense of control present at her house was oppressive for her, her three sisters, and her big brother. Her behavior and choices deteriorated as she moved further into adolescence. I used to feel sorry that her parents seemed so much more like police officers than friends.

I had another friend whose house was a vacuum. I never ran into a parental limit of any kind there. In fact, if we wanted no supervision, his house was the place we chose. Every now and then his mother would be there, but she seemed to be making a social call rather than supervising her son. My friend's house was a "safe place" to get away with some things, but there was also something very empty and "unsafe" about it.

179

As I thought about how to begin this chapter on adolescence, the word that kept coming to me was *balance*. As I look back, I'm most grateful for the balance my parents displayed in my teen years. More than anything else, adolescence requires this balance from a parent. Consider the balancing act between the following extremes:

- A teen who thinks she "knows everything" but comes home sobbing after her best friend shuns her at school
- A teen who is "invulnerable" but experiences up-and-down emotions
- A teen who is fiercely independent but constantly cries for help
- A teen who possesses a sexually mature body but is absolutely ignorant of its use, its dangers, and its true fulfillment
- A teen who is glaringly ignorant but rejects all authority
- A teen who has the incredible ability to change from a strong adult one moment to a vulnerable child the next
- Your own conflicting feelings of wanting to be in control and wanting your child to be independent
- Your being so angry at someone one hour and so in love the next
- Parenting and at the same time preparing your teen for no parent

In this chapter we will take a look at what's going on inside an adolescent and what's going to be required of you.

The Big Picture

To really understand adolescence, you need to stand back and understand first the big picture of how a child develops into an adult. Then you will understand adolescence as something both essential and important.

Remember infancy? (You would probably trade in your teenager's rock music for the crying that irritated you so!) Infancy was a time of learning to trust and depend on others. It was a time to take in love and care, a time for your infant to find out that others can meet his needs and to allow them to be met.

Then came the first step of independence. The toddler has had enough dependency for one life and says that it's time to "be a person of my own." The strong will emerges. Independence emerges. And the child finds it exhilarating as well as terrifying. He loves standing up to you and being his own person, yet ten minutes later can't function without you. Your limits remind him that he is not in control of everything, and slowly he learns to get in control of himself.

Soon after, he learns right from wrong and has to process his own failures and feelings of not being "good enough." He also learns that you aren't the perfect parent, and he learns to accept and work with someone who is also not "good enough." Forgiveness becomes a reality. Anger toward and love of the same person is a developmental milestone. He learns that there is not a "good mom" and a "bad mom." Or a "good me" and a "bad me." There is a "good and bad me" and a "good and bad you." He is building frustration tolerance with himself and others. And that milestone gives him the ability to be imperfect and have good relationships with imperfect people—a skill that serves him for life.

A little later, beginning in elementary school, he learns about being part of a social group. He learns the group's mores and the skills he needs to have friends and belong to a larger group called a community. This community requires him to perform certain tasks, play certain games, have certain skills. He learns these tasks, games, and skills so that he can be a part of the community.

Then he puts all of this together into what is looking more and more like a complete person and less like a child. He thinks more about things, asks more involved questions, and ponders at a deeper level. His skill level increases in many areas and, in some areas, may even surpass your own.

And then it happens. He hits thirteen and goes crazy. Or so it seems to you. Parents ask themselves and others:

"What happened to my nice kid? We were such good
    buddies."
"She used to be friendly, and now she is so moody."
"We have never fought like this before."
"Why does he seem to pull away from us?"
"What happened to all the morals we taught him?"

It can sometimes seem as if someone came one day, took
your child to another planet, and left you this new one instead.
Or maybe you still have the same kid, but she has been infected
with a whole host of insecurities that were never there before.
What in the world is going on?

The easy answer is that all of those things that we just
reviewed are back on the table for a final rewrite. Adolescence
is a time when all of the past developmental issues are reworked
in a different context. Instead of developing these qualities while
he is still "under" the parent, your teenager is working out those
issues in the context of independence in preparation for adulthood. Therefore two things are happening. First, he is going
through the issues in a different, more independent way. Second, the issues are open to reworking and repair if he missed
them the first time around. Here is the list again:

- Trust and dependency
- Independence and autonomy
- Limits and authority
- Living with and accepting imperfection in self and others
- Frustration tolerance
- Social group demands and interpersonal skills
- Talents, abilities, and interests

The bad news is that you thought you were finished with
these issues, but you aren't. The good news is that you have a
second chance to fix things that need fixing, and better than that,
you have an adult emerging with whom you can experience a
whole new relationship. Adolescence, for all of its parenting
trials, can be a very rewarding time. If you know what to watch

out for, it can be one of the best times you have ever had with your soon-to-be-adult child.

Let's look at each of these developmental functions in the adolescent years.

Trust and Dependency

The first time around, your children learned trust and dependency out of desperate need. Infants are alone and demanding, and they know it. They could not care less about being independent. In fact, they hate it. They want Mommy all the time, so responding to their dependency is pretty simple.

In teenagers, it is more complicated. The trust and dependency of teenagers are now going through major changes. Teenagers have to learn to depend and trust all over again in some major ways. If the groundwork was laid in infancy and early childhood and not interrupted by some trauma, teens have a good foundation to do it all over again in some different ways.

First, there is the issue of trusting you and your spouse. While infants look to you for connection and soothing, adolescents look to you for understanding. For sure, the connection and soothing will still be important aspects, but they happen differently. Adolescents feel connected when they feel understood, as opposed to feeling physically close. They feel connected when you understand that they don't necessarily want to do things the same way you do, or that the trauma they are experiencing might seem small to the rest of the world but to them is everything.

I had lunch with a youth pastor who specializes in high school ministry.

"How's it going?" I asked him as he sat down.

"I never will get used to it, even though I see it every day," he replied.

"What's that?"

"The experience of seeing the whole range of emotion in teenagers for very different reasons. I just had meetings with two teenage girls this morning. You could not have told the difference in what was happening in their lives by their reactions. Both were inconsolable and distraught. Both were traumatized. Both burst out crying when they came into my office. But get this: The first girl's grandmother had just died. The second girl had just found out that her braces wouldn't be off in time for the prom!"

Obviously, the second girl was going to have to go through a few steps of maturity to learn what's really important in life. But to teenagers, everything can feel extremely important, and when a parent devalues their current crisis or feelings, trust is broken. Validation of their experience is very important, and such affirmation comes less from lectures than from empathy. A "Gosh, I can see you are really sad about that. It must have been really important to you" can go a lot further than "How can you be upset about something so trivial?" Empathize with teenagers, and they are more likely to see their circumstance as trivial faster than if they have to fight to have their own feelings.

They will be asking a bigger question as well about trust with you. "Can I lean on you without your robbing me of my independence?" We will look at autonomy in a moment, but this is a big issue for trust in general. Teenagers want to trust you, to be able to come to you, to look to you for guidance. But if they are not able to do that without being controlled, they will look for someone else to trust.

Shelly had the beginnings of an eating disorder, called bulimia. She was bingeing and purging. Her mother did not know about her problem, but knew that something was wrong. As Shelly began to open up to me in a counseling session, I found that there had been a recent rift with her mother. They had not had these kinds of communication problems before her mid-teens. But recently, Shelly was moody and withdrawn, and her mother was feeling slighted.

"After all I've done for her" was the emotional theme from Mom.

Shelly's version of the rift was a lot different and had a lot of validity. As she summed it up one day, "I feel like I can't talk to my mom without her telling me what I ought to do, or how I ought to think. She can't just listen and understand." The closeness that they had once had was changing as Shelly wanted her own thoughts and space. Her mother could not resist the impulse to try to control Shelly's life.

Trust for teens is also built through a parent's genuineness and congruence. Teenagers can spot a fake, a hypocrite, or a role player as fast and as accurately as radar can nail a speeding car. When you are not being real, being true, having integrity with your own agenda and feelings, or being honest, your teens will see it. And they will not trust you, especially in the spiritual area. To put forth God as a way of controlling kids for a parent's own agenda is spiritual abuse. Teens believe people who seem real and honest. They want people who are congruent with what they are saying.

As you can share real things in real ways and can be there for your teenagers as a background security against which they find out who they are, you will likely establish meaningful connection and intimacy. Do not be dismayed at the fluctuations they go through in that process. Remember, they are asking the question all over again: Whom can I trust?

Do not be dismayed at their emerging tendency to put more trust into others than you. This can also be a way of establishing independence. I know one adolescent who currently tells her mother "wonderful things" she has learned and totally forgets that her mother told her that same thing before her new source did. But to get it on her own is more important to the daughter than to get it from Mom. Your teen is learning to trust people with important issues all over again, but she will do some of this away from you—with friends or with another adult. Teens will often find an adult mentor, such as a youth leader or someone else's parent. This is a normal and healthy thing. Do not let jealousy get in the way of your teen's need to reach out to a world larger than yours.

Teens are also learning to trust in the romantic realm. If you have not already seen it, that first "love" is on its way. They are expanding the trust you taught them early into new arenas. Watch, and observe. See if they are making good choices in whom they are trusting and getting close to. Make sure you have done some good teaching and have had some good discussions on boundaries in sex and dating. By the time they are ready to date, there should be no questions about morals and safety.

Save your editorials for significant issues, but at least in the beginning, help her examine her relationships through questions. Ask about the new boy she is hanging around with. What is it like to be around him? How does he make her feel? Does she like feeling that way? How does she feel about his having no spiritual life? Does she miss sharing that part of herself with someone?

Many times parents will lecture a teenage daughter early on in a relationship about why a certain boy is not good for her to trust or to get close to. Don't get us wrong: Sometimes limits have to be set. But more often, what is better is that your daughter comes to her own conclusion that this person is not trustworthy. And someone can only do that if she gets in touch with how the relationship really makes her feel. The above questions help in that regard. If you just lecture her, she sees you as the problem and fails to see the problem in the relationship. The control issue gets in the way of her seeing the reality of the relationship and who she is trusting.

We have all seen teens make horrible choices because they were so caught up in the control issue with a parent that they were unable to see what they were doing. As God tells us, "But solid food is for the mature, who because of practice have their senses trained to discern good and evil" (Hebrews 5:14 NASB). Their practice in getting to know different people will teach them if you help teenagers to see what their experience really is. Help them to get in touch with their own senses.

Of course, you need to set boundaries on how much you will let them learn on their own. Some relationships are so destructive that you might have to limit them or even forbid them altogether. This is a difficult thing to do and rarely goes smoothly. But if there is a danger to your child having a certain friend or being in a certain group, you still must protect him where his own senses don't. This is part of what he is trusting you to do, no matter what he says. But as much as is possible, stay away from control issues up to that point, and if you have to go there, make sure that you give the reality reasons. "I fear for your life if you hang around that person, and I don't want to lose you to drugs."

Independence and Autonomy

One parent described adolescence as the terrible twos all over again, but this time in a bigger body. We personally don't see either time period as "terrible," but each one can be a time full of difficulty if you don't recognize the important stage of independence, separateness, and autonomy that a child is going through. In the "twos," toddlers are moving away from the early dependency of infancy. In the teens, children are moving away from their lifelong dependency of leaning on parents for a lot of functioning. They are looking to

- Think for themselves and have their own opinions
- Question, evaluate, and choose values
- Follow their own desires and goals
- Build skills and abilities
- Look ahead
- Develop their own spirituality
- Find their own ways of making money
- Have parents available to them while they are working all of this out

These are all good things. Participate in your adolescent's emerging autonomy by being proactive. Many parents just back off, wait for the testing of limits to begin, broaden the boundaries. In short, they put all the planning on the adolescent and then try to prevent the developmental path from working! Since you know that in these years teenagers are learning to "guard and manage" themselves, be proactive and develop a plan with them for giving them more autonomy.

Friends of mine took their thirteen-year-old daughter on a weekend retreat to talk about the future. We had discussed the growth paradigm in my book *Changes That Heal,* and they thought that the tasks explained in that book would be a good map for taking their daughter through adolescence. The paradigm talks about four developmental steps that everyone must take to grow up: bonding, setting boundaries, integrating good and bad, and becoming an adult. They basically told her something like the following:

"Sarah, you're thirteen now and entering your teens. These years are an important time of growing up into the person you will become. We want to help you in that process. When we thought what we would like for you to possess when you leave us in five years, we came up with the following:

1. We want you to have the ability to connect with God and with other people in a significant way. We want you to have close relationships with good people who love you and do not hurt you.
2. We want you to have a good sense of self-control and personal boundaries. We want you to be in control of yourself and not for others to be in control of you. We want you to be self-directed and able to say no to things in yourself and from others that are not good for you or that you do not want.
3. We want you to be able to be comfortable with who you are, both good and bad. We want you to own your good parts and work on your weak areas. We want you to understand the process of confession and forgiveness. We want you to be able to face problems and solve them, including your sin and failure.
4. We want you to have a good sense of your talents, abilities, opinions, desires, values, and sexuality. We want you to think about these things and to choose wisely. We don't want them just to be ours, but for you to own them as yours.

Given all of that, Sarah, how can we work together to make these years a time when you are developing this kind of character? What do you need from us? What do you think we can expect from you in this process? What experiences and resources do we need to provide for these things to happen? How do we need to help and protect you as well?"

And then the parents and Sarah spend a lot of time working out those issues as a team. It was really neat to hear about. I have been impressed with the depth of their relationship with Sarah and the way they at the same time have partnered in her independence.

Being a partner in your teenagers' independence is a good way to look at this issue. They will establish independence one way or another. They are wired by God to do that. So it is better if you become a partner instead of an adversary in this process with them. If you become a partner, they will need you and look to you. If you become an adversary, you will lose them, and they will lose the ability to grow into independence in a way connected to love and authority.

Partnering in independence and autonomy means to think always about your children guarding and managing themselves at the appropriate level. Give them enough space to fail, and then manage the failure with nurture, empowerment, support, discipline, and correction. Or, when they succeed, give them more. Show them that responsible use of freedom leads to more freedom. As Jesus taught, "Well done, good and faithful servant! You have been faithful with a few things; I will put you in charge of many things. Come and share your master's happiness!" (Matthew 25:21, 23). Faithfulness in a little leads to receiving more. Here are some areas where your teenagers are likely to demand more freedom and control over their lives:

- More freedom to go places and stay out later
- More freedom to do what they please without your being there all the time
- More freedom in choosing things they like instead of what you like

- Freedom to question things you have taught them and make up their own minds
- Freedom to pursue their own interests
- Control over their likes and dislikes
- More control over their spiritual life

When these desires emerge, remember that your goal is to use them to manage the process of independence in a way that leads to teenagers being able to manage themselves. Give them the freedom within limits and require them to use it responsibly. Do not see every drive to be independent as a testing of limits, although testing will come. See each incident as an opportunity to find out what kind of freedom they can manage and what kind they cannot. Do not give them more than they can manage, for your role as guardian and manager kicks in when they are in danger. But at the same time, do not restrict their freedom when they are able to manage it. To the extent that you are guarding and managing them in areas where they are showing faithfulness and responsibility, *you are redundant and unnecessary.*

Expect them to do some things that you don't like and that don't make sense, just to express their independence from you. A good friend of mine was torn between giving his son permission to get an earring and forbidding him to get one. We talked it over, and I asked about the important areas of life. Was he doing his chores? Was he making his grades? Was he pursuing his spiritual life? Did he pick good friends? The answers were all yes.

"Your son is doing well," I told my friend. "He wants to show you that he is different from you by doing something that you would never do. In my view, this is a pretty safe area for him to rebel against being just like you. I would rather let him prove to himself that he is his own person with an earring than with drugs. Let him do it."

It was traumatic for this macho dad. He could hardly stomach the looks of his son with an earring, even though in reality, in California that particular item is about as rebellious as a necktie in Michigan. For this particular dad, it was a difficult pill to swallow, but to his credit, he swallowed it. He did not get caught up in the small things his son did to reveal his independence when he was being faithful in the big things. Some battles are worth fighting, and some are not. Harmless ones designed to show independence are not.

Look for individual expression in music, clothes, hobbies, political views, overall appearance, and the like. If their choices do not get them into danger, let it go. It's a natural drive for them to say, "I know you don't like it, but I do!" In most cases their peers will enforce the limits of what is okay and what is not. If they go too far, they will run into trouble in their own social circles. But remember, their norms are different from yours.

If they begin to make unsafe choices that could lead to moral or physical danger, it's time for limits. Funky dress is okay, even if you as a parent don't like it. Over-revealing dress is not okay; it implies promiscuity and gives a message to others that your child is open to dangerous activity. Dress that is so offensive that it shows the world that the child doesn't care to fit in anywhere is not okay; it may indicate a significant problem that needs to be addressed, such as depression or isolation.

Choosing their own friends that you are not crazy about is okay. But associating with dangerous characters who could lead your child into drug and alcohol abuse, gang participation, or other dangerous activities is not okay. You may have to step in and restrict that friendship. But if there is no moral or other danger, the child is the one who is going to have to put up with the friend, not you.

In the spiritual area, your children might try to show independence as well. Do not get into a power struggle over God. Teenagers may reject God just to show you that they still have freedom and choices. Show them God. Live out his life, his love, and his truth. Expose teens to good activities and teaching. Get them involved in a good youth group with good youth leaders who are fun and have things going that they like as part of their spiritual ministry. Give teenagers an opportunity, but remember that they have to make their own choices. Very often, another person such as a youth pastor or a friend is much more influential with a teen than a parent who is getting into spiritual control battles. Pray for your teen, show him how, but do not try to control him into faith. Remember what the apostle Paul said: "It was for freedom that Christ set us free; therefore keep standing firm and do not be subject again to a yoke of slavery" (Galatians 5:1 NASB). If God is not making your teenager a spiritual slave, neither should you.

In short, you *want* your adolescents to develop independence. If they don't, you will still be bailing them out when they are forty. This is the time to help them develop independence in the right way. Give them areas in which they can be different from you *that do not involve values*. If you allow them to do this, they won't have to sacrifice more important areas of life to show you that they are their own person.

Limits and Authority

It is important to let your child become independent and more autonomous. But remember, *they are not there yet!* You are still around to protect them and manage them until they are ready. The problem is that *they think they are ready now!* They are big and grown, with engines raring and ready to go. If you ask them, they know everything. They can handle it! "Stop treating me like a child!" is a cry that you may hear often. But to some degree, they still are children until they reach adulthood. So, until that day, you and your limits are still needed.

There is an inherent conflict in this arrangement. As Paul said, the experience to them is like slavery: "What I am saying is that as long as the heir is a child, he is no different from a slave, although he owns the whole estate. He is subject to guardians and trustees until the time set by his father" (Galatians 4:1–2). Your teenagers have all the equipment, but they are still under your management. And while that's necessary, they don't like it. But just because they don't like it doesn't make it unnecessary. You and your limits are really needed.

You still have to give them limits and enforce the limits even as they want more and more freedom. As we saw above, you *must* be giving them more freedom. But freedom only has meaning within certain boundaries. Your job is to give them boundaries that protect them in reality when they get past their own ability to manage themselves faithfully in moral and interpersonal matters:

1. **Reality limits**. Reality limits are limits in areas where there is real danger. Sex and drugs, for example, can kill you. So can gangs and drunk driving. Your limits prevent them from falling into danger. Other examples include flunking out of school and wrecking one's future career and choices. The answer to requests for freedom in these areas is "Never."

2. **"Past-their-ability" limits.** These limits involve no danger, but the child may not have shown responsibility in a certain area. Heeding curfew, taking care of possessions, managing money, using Dad's car, having parents pay for another expensive hobby (that the child drops out of after a few weeks) are all examples of past-their-ability limits; these privileges should be earned through responsible behavior. The answer to requests for freedom in these areas is "When you show you are able to handle that freedom."

3. **Moral, spiritual, and interpersonal limits.** These limits develop the character needed for success in life and relationships. Limits that prevent things like lying, cheating, stealing, promiscuity, and disregard for authority protect a child's life later by building character now. Limits that make children aware of spiritual values let them know that they are not God and must ultimately submit to him. Limits that prevent children from disrespecting and being mean to others protect their relationships later. Love is paramount. This may include how they treat a sibling, a friend, a boyfriend or girlfriend, or you. For example, when they talk back to you in a disrespectful

way, do not allow it. Have them communicate openly, but respecting you as a person.

When you are thinking of imposing limits on your adolescent, ask yourself, "What is the danger here?" Think of limits in the areas of reality danger, responsibility and faithfulness, and interpersonal relationships. If one of these areas is violated, set limits and discipline.

In the next chapter we will discuss specific things that many parents of teenagers ask about.

——— Eleven ———

Dealing with Specific Teenage Issues

We are strong believers in principles. That is why the Bible is so timeless. Principles can tell you how to handle almost any situation. So, we usually do not talk a lot about "how to handle" specifics. Children create more specifics than we could ever cover! But some specific situations are very common in dealing with teens. So, here are some of them and how our principles apply.

Music

Let your children have their own musical choices in terms of style, beat, kind, and decibel level. Your parents did not like the Beatles, either. You might have to intervene when the content gets into nonlife themes like suicide, hurtful sexuality, and violence. What your child is listening to either affects him or expresses something for him. Either way, listening to music with nonlife themes is a bad sign. Get involved and find what the music means to him, and we hope you can lead him out of it. If not, you will have to restrict this death influence.

In addition, part of respecting others is abiding by the rule of treating others as one would want to be treated. If your son is keeping others awake or creating a disturbance, this is not okay.

Hair, Clothes, Earrings, Appearance

In general, a teen's body and appearance are hers. Just as no one tells you what to wear and not wear, no one should tell her, either. But there are exceptions here as well. We have freedom of speech, but we can't yell "Bomb!" on an airplane. It is the same for dress. Your child needs to learn the limits of appropriate dress for certain situations. See what is normal for various situations, and give her freedom within those limits. This will help her later in life. Besides this, don't sweat the small stuff.

If, as we mentioned in the previous chapter, things get out of hand to the point where her clothing choices could lead to trouble, you must have limits. Promiscuous dress, antisocial dress, and appearance that connotes death themes or antisociety themes are signs of trouble. First seek to understand what this dress means to your child. Find out what she is expressing. But keep the limit if there is danger. And before you proceed, reread the chapter on the ingredients of grace and truth—you are going to need both! Remember to say no and empathize.

Earrings and hair are usually not a big deal unless they suggest some alternative lifestyle, which could mean trouble. "To the pure, all things are pure." Find out what the meaning is before jumping in. If it's independence, fine. If it's rebellion against life or morals, that's another story.

Curfew

Curfews are probably different in different communities and regions of the country. Talk to other parents and find out what kids do after certain hours. Don't restrict them in a way that socially isolates them, but make sure their time is limited in some way, keeping in mind danger and moral realities.

It is sometimes dangerous to be out past certain hours, and in some instances, a teenager has no good reason to be where he is in the first place. But if a child is responsible, has a good reason, and keeps you informed, be flexible. A limit is good and absolutely necessary; it orders and structures the child. But remember, the Sabbath was made for man, not man for the Sabbath. Or, in other words, the limit was made for your child, not your child for the limit.

Spirituality

Teens should have choices about their spiritual life, but you need to expose them to God and your faith and beliefs. Up to the late teen years, we would suggest doing everything possible to get them to attend church and Sunday school. (In college they are going to do whatever they want.) But do give them a choice. Maybe they hate the style of worship service or the youth group at your church. Let them pick their own if they want. What a victory, if they go! It really doesn't matter where they go as long as the church is legitimate.

Don't turn religion into a control issue. My parents had a good policy. After age fifteen, they said I (Dr. Cloud) did not have to go to church if I didn't want to, but that I couldn't do anything else. They said something like, "Our family reserves this time for God. You don't have to go to church if you don't want to, but you can't do anything else, either." We never had a problem. There was no control, just a limit, and I chose church.

Spirituality, however, is *much* more than church. Day-to-day we live out our spiritual values of love, faithfulness, honesty, compassion, forgiveness, stewardship of talents and life, and hope. First, live out these values yourself, or your teenagers will hate your hypocrisy—your saying one thing and doing another. But, second, set limits and intervene when your children do not live them out. Discipline them with consequences when they do not show these values. This is exactly what God and life are going to do later. Both God and reality are going to show them that these values are not just rules; they are life itself. Not possessing them comes at a price.

Sex and Substances

Sex, alcohol, marijuana (and harder drugs) can wreak havoc in a person's life, and these are traditional problem areas for teens. The best medicine is prevention. Give your teenagers good education about all three. Be positive about sexuality, but serious about the limits. As much as possible, make the limits relate to reality. Contracting a sexually transmitted disease, being used by a sexual partner, destroying relationships (both future and present), becoming pregnant, and disintegrating a personality are all reality reasons for God's limits. Guilt and shame are not. Explain these reasons, and connect your teens with good youth role models with whom they can identify. (The National Institute of Youth Ministry is a good example of such a group.)

If you find out that your child is sexually active, find out why. In a home of good moral teaching, sexual activity is many times a sign of something else. Is the child depressed, discouraged, in a control battle, lonely, without boundaries and unable to say "no," subject to "rigid" morality, or something else? Do not see the violation only. Temptation to do "bad" often comes in the context of the absence of something "good." If a teen feels unloved or powerless, for example, she may choose sex to make her feel wanted and powerful. Or, it may be a way of getting back at a rigid parent. Find out what is missing.

With substances, the same is true. Children need models and reality education. Get them exposed to good teaching and information. Any use of drugs is a significant issue and should not be overlooked. Experimentation with alcohol is not unusual, but make sure that you take this seriously as well—especially if driving is involved—for it may be more than experimentation. Talk about it if your teenager confesses misuse or abuse, but still keep the limit and consequences. What you show at home is a very big part of the picture. If you are being responsible, they are more likely to be as well. If they are not, impose the necessary limits and restrictions. By all means, give them a way out. Let them know that they can call you at anytime from anywhere if they need a ride home or an escape from a difficult situation or some other kind of help.

If you do have a child who is using illegal substances and who is not stopping with a warning from you, treat it as a serious problem until you find out that your child has stopped. The family with an addiction is usually the last one to see it clearly. Get help from someone who knows how to treat teen addiction. In some cases you may have to tell the child that he cannot continue to live at home, that you do not allow drugs in your house, and he therefore has to go away until he is drug free.

Studies

By and large, your children should be managing their own study time by the time they become teenagers. You manage the grades. Figure out what is reasonable to expect from each child and then expect it. Take deviations from your expectations as a sign that they are not managing their school life by themselves, and give them consequences. If that does not work, you may have to talk to the school principal or a teacher. But in the beginning, let your kids manage the "how" if they can. For example, it doesn't matter so much when and where they do their homework if they are getting it done. Become involved only when their performance shows that you need to.

If there is a problem, as in the matter of sex or drugs, take it as a sign that something else may be going on. Falling grades may be a symptom of depression, social problems, school problems, or other issues. Find out the "why" before you give the discipline. Remember, "He who gives an answer before he hears, it is folly and shame to him" (Proverbs 18:13 NASB).

In all of these areas and others as well, the message is simple and the ingredients are clear. The message is:

1. Some things are dangerous; stay away from them, or you will die.
2. Some things are not wise; do not do them, or you will lose.
3. Some things are not moral; avoid them, and you will win.
4. You are in charge of all of the above until you prove that you cannot be, and then we or the law will intervene.

The ingredients are:

1. *Grace.* In all ways, show that you are for your children and not against them. Empower them to do the right thing, and do not become adversarial. Give them "no condemnation" (Romans 8:1).
2. *Truth.* In all ways, you show them what is right and then enforce that with correction, limits, and consequences.

Keep the truth with reality consequences and not emotional ones like guilt, anger, or fear.

3. *Time.* This is a process. They are learning to do your job of guarding and managing themselves. This takes time and experience.

4. *Flexibility.* This is a dance. You and your child are both changing your roles—you, into less of a parent; your child, into more of an adult. The roles and individuals must always be changing and not rigid.

Living with and Accepting Imperfection in Themselves and Others

Teens have totally unrealistic standards of themselves and sometimes others. They go up and down with their own failures and successes. A pimple can be the stimulus for a nervous breakdown. A missed goal in soccer can announce the label "loser." Help them to accept themselves as they are with a goal of always getting better.

The best defense against imperfection is love. To the degree that your children feel loved, they will be able to accept their imperfections. Do not devalue their feelings, but empathize. Give them lots of positive feedback on their strengths and talents.

As we said earlier, this step is one of the process. It involves being open about negatives and failures and then facing them with grace and truth. As your teens test the limits, fail, and sin, make sure that you face all of those issues with lots of grace. To the extent that you shame and condemn them, they may develop a good-bad split. They will begin to show the good child on the exterior and hide the bad stuff from you. Make it safe enough for them to bring it all to you and integrate.

Especially important in this process is your acceptance of their feelings. They may go through extremes of rage and depression at times. Remember that your job is to be big enough to not react to their reactions. You don't have to become a teenager to deal with one! Stay calm, and give them empathy and understanding, even when they are hating you. Don't allow attack, but accept their feelings. Then they will be able to integrate their emotional extremes. Empathize with their heartache and sadness, sexual frustrations, and "less than holy attitudes," and then contain and structure their anger. Above all, let them know that forgiveness is always available, no matter what they do. As the apostle Paul said, "Be kind and compassionate to one another, forgiving each other, just as in Christ God forgave you" (Ephesians 4:32).

Frustration Tolerance and Delay of Gratification

A client of mine divorced when his son was fourteen, and he and his former wife had shared custody. He had always had strong limits on the boy, but his ex-wife had allowed the boy to have his way much of the time. As a result of his mother's lack of limits, the boy felt entitled, thinking that he could have whatever he wanted without having to work or wait. He dropped out of college in his sophomore year, and his mother continued to bail him out.

When I ran into this client the other day, he told me that his son, now twenty-five, had just inherited some money from a relative for the purpose of furthering his education. The day his son received the money, guess what? Did he send it to the college of his choice? Hardly! He went out and bought a new car. Waiting and working were not in his vocabulary. The dad was grief stricken, knowing that the rest of this young man's life was potentially going to go the same route.

In the teen years, delay of gratification is an important quality. It comes from a parent having limits and the proper stance toward pleasure. Pleasure is good! Teach your children that. But for pleasure that lasts, we have to work first. Wait for the best. To teach your children to learn to wait, make sure that you limit what is limitable so they will limit what is more intangible. For example, if you want them to wait for sex, which you cannot control, teach them to wait for a new piece of sports equipment until they earn half the money. Teach them to wait for a car until they earn part of it. Or teach them to use your car only as they pay some of the expenses. Teach them that they can go on the ski trip this Christmas if they earn good grades.

The content is not important. What is important is that they learn to delay gratification until they do their part. Contain the rage and screams of "That's not fair. Bill is getting one!" Empathize with them. Tell them, "I know it's hard." Encourage and help them along the way, without enabling them by bailing them out and making life seem easier than it really is. Help them learn to work first and play later. The principle will serve them for a lifetime.

Social Group Demands and Interpersonal Skills

Your teenagers are going to enter the world of dating and seeking to fit in socially to a greater degree than ever. This is normal, and you should encourage it. (We disagree with a "dating is bad" approach that is becoming popular.) Watch them, and look for the normal socialization process. They should be involved somewhere in larger group activities, whatever their own tastes dictate. Dating and opposite-sex relationships should be happening as well. Also, healthy teens have a clan that they run around with, the usual kids you are used to seeing. Get to know their friends, and be a friend to them. Make your home a friendly place where they can hang out and have freedom and warmth. The home that is a teen gathering place speaks volumes to the child about having his own life and yet integrating with the family.

All of these are healthy signs of a teen's emerging abilities as a social person. But there will be periods of difficulty. Watch for them so that you can help. If something is absent, ask about it. Maybe they don't feel likable, so they do not venture out. They may need some help or counseling. Maybe they have had a heartbreak that they're not telling you about. First, ask yourself why? Maybe there is a good reason they do not feel as if they can talk to you. Address that first. But after that, try to help them get past the hurdle that they are feeling at present. There is probably some growth step that they need to make. Sometimes you might even notice the problem first. If you see character patterns in your child that are costing her friendships or boyfriends, let her know. You are doing her a favor by making her face it instead of blaming or withdrawing.

Talents, Abilities, and Interests

We have talked a lot about talents, abilities, and interests, but in the teen years, focus on a few important things in helping your children develop.

1. Make sure your children's interests are theirs, not yours. Their drive to be separate will overshadow their drive to succeed, and they may quit something that they are good at just to get separate from you.

2. Support your children in what they do choose. Encourage, but don't get too caught up in results, just the process. Whether they win is not as important as what they are learning along the way.

3. Require your children to stick it out, especially if you're paying for it. Sometimes, if a child has a history of being responsible, it's okay for him to quit something new if he discovers he really doesn't like it after trying it for a while. I was like that with swimming. I hated it, so I quit. But I had a history of finishing other seasons of sports and not dropping out. When I took piano, it was a different story. I had started it, and I hated it. But my parents made me finish because to run from it would have been avoiding the growth task of finishing something I had committed to. I had agreed to a year, and they made me finish. I hated it, but I'm glad they forced me to stick it out. It helps me write books now when the going gets tough! Don't ask me to play piano—I am horrible at it. But I did learn something in the process.

4. Expose your children to a lot of choices, and to an extent, help in creating opportunities if you can. We don't

believe in paying for everything for a teen. But sometimes, for a teen who is paying his part, you might help
out just to get him the exposure along the way.

5. Share activities and skills with your children. This gets
   them involved in watching how you handle hobbies and
   fun as well as new skills. Learn to ski together or roller
   blade or bicycle. It is fun and a good bonding experience
   as well as a chance to model the process.

The Result

If you do all of the above, then you will have a new person
at the end of the process. You will have a friend for life—one
of whom you can be proud, and whom you can watch unfold
as God directs his steps into the future. Your job is over. What
did you do?

You taught your children that all the things you had been
teaching them were one day for them to manage. You taught
them that your job as guardian and manager was just temporary,
and that what you were doing was just showing them how to
do what they would have to do later: guard and manage themselves. And if they can now do that, you have done well. As the
song says, "Give them roots, and give them wings." You have
given them what they need to go out into the world on their own:
character.

In the teen years you have given them the process of freedom, discipline, love, support, and forgiveness that helped them
to become their own people. That is something to be proud of
as you let go and retire from your job as parent. Congratulations!

Part Four

Dealing with Special Circumstances

───── Twelve ─────

Understanding Temperaments

I finally solved the problem of Russell being so hardheaded and Lindsay so easygoing," said my (Dr. Townsend's) friend Maureen. "I found out that they have different temperaments, so I've accepted that instead of fighting it. That helps take the pressure off. Now my only concern is that Russell gets in trouble a lot, and people take advantage of Lindsay. So is that just their lot in life?"

Much has been written about understanding people's temperaments. Temperament has to do with certain categories of inborn traits that cause people to respond differently to life. This may include tendencies toward introversion or extroversion and activity or passivity, for example. Somewhat like personality theories, temperament theories seek to help explain the ways people are different.

Many parents wonder about how to deal with temperament types. If a child responds poorly to you, is it temperament or rebellion? Does the parent accept and adapt to it, or correct the child? Maureen felt that she had to work around her son's willfulness and her daughter's compliance. She was afraid that dealing with these might harm them, as God obviously designed them that way.

Temperament Is Not Character

We have several beliefs about temperament. First, we believe that children do have differing styles and traits. Individual differences, from energy level to academic interests, simply make up your child's unique soul. He is "fearfully and wonderfully made" by God (Psalm 139:14), and the particular mixture that makes him "him" gives him his own special potential to make contributions to the lives of others.

However, temperament is not the same as character. On the one hand, temperament is a style of relating to the world. It is inborn, and it has its own strengths and weaknesses. Some kids make a million friends a day, for example, and some have a few intensely loyal comrades.

Character, on the other hand, is not a style. It is a set of necessary abilities to function in the world, and we are universally responsible to develop all the character traits in ourselves. Unlike temperament, we can't say, "Well, my son has a detached style, and my daughter has an irresponsible style. Guess that's the way it is." *Character is neither an option nor an alternative. It is a requirement for survival.*

We feel strongly that character development should make allowances for differences in temperament, but character and temperament are not equal. Character comes first, style second. To explain what we mean, consider how you order dinner from a menu. You need the appropriate amounts of the basic food groups: so many ounces of meat, so many of vegetables, fruits, and grains. If you decide you have a meat style and eat nothing else, the consequences are likely to be cholesterol and heart problems. But once you have submitted to the basic food parameters, you have many choices of style and taste.

In the same way, you need to help your child mature in all of the character traits we have written about in this book. But take his individuality into consideration as you do. This way his burden isn't excessively heavy. For example, a child who is more sensitive and intuitive may need less direct correction than a turbo-charged one. The first might respond with a look or gentle word, and to go further could be hurtful. The second may need many clear, direct corrections, with consequences quickly charging in like the cavalry to get the same message. But *whatever the temperament, the task of learning responsibility is the same for both.* Although styles may vary, all kids need to take ownership of their lives.

One of the difficulties of parenting is that while your child needs your help in all areas, you most likely won't excel at all. You have a responsibility to help your child grow in all the character traits; however, your ability in each area is not the same. For example, you may have strengths in attachment, but have difficulty with limits. Or you may be great at competency, but your own perfectionism hinders your ability to help your child deal with reality. So you may need to work on some issues yourself. We can't overemphasize the importance of finding help from others for your weak areas. This is one of the ways we can carry each other's burdens (Galatians 6:2).

How to Tell the Difference

It is sometimes difficult to tell if a problem is temperament-influenced or character-based, as the outworking of each is similar. For example, a child may intrude on others, interrupt, and be pushy. This problem could be driven by a more energetic temperament. Or it could be caused by a lack of internalized structure-building and consequences. It could even be Attention Deficit Disorder. How does a parent tell the difference?

Obviously, getting an expert's opinion, as from a teacher or child therapist, can be helpful, especially if you suspect a medical or psychological condition. Given that, however, there is a basic difference in temperament-influenced behaviors and character-based issues. *When character issues are resolved, the remaining temperament issues don't tend to be a major problem.* People can have very different temperaments and still be well within normal ranges of psychological assessments. But great disparities in character often result in great differences in functioning and problems in life.

So if you see a tendency you are concerned about, a good rule of thumb is to investigate it first as a character issue. For example, if your child is like the pushy child above, check out the following:

- Is she seeking relationship the only way she knows how?

- Is she unaware of how her behavior affects others?
- Is she testing people to see if they can stand her?
- Is she operating without any consequences?
- Does she provoke others as a way to make them set limits with her?
- Is she afraid of people seeing her vulnerability, and reacting against it?

Most of the time the answer lies in character, especially with disruptive problems. Differences in temperament don't tend to be as extreme.

So What?

However, we have a little bad news here. Let's suppose your child's struggles are zero percent character and one hundred percent temperament. Suppose it's all inborn, and therefore God has either caused or allowed it. For example, say your daughter has a genetic predisposition to withdraw from relationship, and she has great difficulty getting close to people. It is through neither your child's nor your wrongdoing that she has this trait.

So what? The bad news is that even though her temperament is not her fault, she is increasingly responsible for dealing with it as she grows up. She will have to deal with her tendency to be introverted and isolate from people. Or compliant and get walked on. Or inwardly-oriented and have trouble paying attention. She will need to learn how to adapt her temperament as much as possible to reality, and not demand the reverse. We disagree with those who would advise her to insist that others change life to fit her style, especially in matters of relationship and responsibility. She will need to make temperament a character-growth issue. This is one of the burdens of maturity.

This is also one of the messages of the Bible. In life we deal not only with problems we have caused, but also with problems not caused by us. Thus, we need to solve problems, not establish blame. Immature people demand justice and reparation for their hurts. Mature people fix the hurts. Just as Paul's "thorn in the flesh" led him to greater maturity in his love for God (2 Corinthians 12:7–10), your child is learning to adapt and thrive in a fallen world.

When do you deal with temperament as a problem, not a "way of being"? Here is the rule: *Deal with temperament when it inhibits growth in attachment, ownership, reality, and all the other character-growth aspects.* When the daydreamer resists coming out of his fantasy world to interact with other children, we do him no favors by allowing him to stay isolated, saying, "Well, you know he needs his creative space." One can be creative and yet be connected to others.

Styles and temperaments can be modified with experience. Research has shown that environment has a powerful effect even on inborn traits. This is a testimony to the redemptive work of God: Our traits don't determine our lives.

The Strong-willed Child

Some parents avoid confronting the strong-willed child's determination to have life his own way. They don't want to squelch his will or discourage him from being decisive. At the same time, they are concerned about helping the child mind them and learn obedience, as this type of kid tends to eat the rules for breakfast.

The strong-willed child's power should end where the family's peace of mind begins. Love, empathy, correction, experience, and consequences are his solution. We have seen many examples where people have been able to make significant changes in their kids' lives using these principles.

— Thirteen —

Parenting on Your Own

Single parents are increasingly common. Whether you never married, are divorced, or are widowed, parenting on your own is very difficult and brings its own set of problems. If this is your situation, our hearts go out to you as you deal with both personal and parenting losses.

God himself understands your struggle. He, too, was a single parent, being divorced from "faithless Israel" (Jeremiah 3:8). And he also raised his children without a spouse. He is "close to the brokenhearted and saves those who are crushed in spirit" (Psalm 34:18).

Ideally, parenting is a two-person job. To help you deal with the reality of your difficult task as a single parent, we have listed below some of the main conditions a two-parent household has the advantage of being able to deal with. This isn't intended to discourage you, but to help you understand what your child needs. Then, with each condition, we will provide suggestions on how you as a single parent can help your child in these areas.

If you and your ex are good coparents, you can fulfill many objectives by working together. Blessed are the children whose parents sacrifice their conflicts to help them mature.

Many good organizations can help single parents in the following areas. If you are the mother of a small child, we strongly encourage you to contact MOPS (Mothers of Preschoolers, Inc.) and become involved in a MOPS group. These groups are designed to support and nurture you as you mother your child. They meet regularly in churches all over the world. Check the information in the back of this book and give them a call. In addition, groups that help men such as PromiseKeepers, and magazines like *Single-Parent Family Magazine* are good resources.

We also recommend *Successful Single Parenting* (Harvest House) by Gary Richmond.

The Conditions

1. Children ideally need two parents to meet their varied needs. Through no fault of their own, single parents generally cannot meet all their child's needs. A second parent can provide what the first one lacks. One parent may be better at connection, while the other is strong on structure. For example, you might be gifted in intuitively knowing how your child feels and where she is hurting, but you may have problems setting and enforcing limits on her school performance.

Become a student of your strengths and weaknesses. Figure out what you don't do well and what deficits need to be filled for your child's development. Form healthy relationships in church, in your neighborhood, and with friends, and ask for their help in areas where you are weak. You want people who are willing to become involved with your child over a significant period of time.

When I (Dr. Townsend) was single and had no kids, I spent regular time with a couple of families who had small children. They had me over to the house numerous times, and I performed a number of Big Brother functions with their children. These relationships were important for me and for them. They helped me stay in touch with the real-life issues that come up in families: creating a safe and loving environment, working through conflict, and being open and honest about struggles. They also helped prepare me for marriage and kids.

You can find such help through friends, church, or community organizations.

2. Children are demanding. One parent can easily be drained and exhausted by the continuous needs of a child. Two parents provide breaks for each other. Some single parents will say, "I really love my kid, but sometimes when I can't get away, I start hating him, and I don't want to."

As your child grows, both you and he will benefit by taking time away from each other. Arrange co-op baby-sitting with other parents. Ask relatives and friends to spell you. You will come back refreshed and looking forward to connecting with your child.

3. *Parenting is basically relationship.* The parent who is in a relationship with a spouse is more able to help her child feel loved when she is herself loved by someone. Not only that, but the child also experiences a model of relationship as he sees parents give to each other what they give him.

Your worst enemies are isolation and self-sufficiency. You need regular, vulnerable contact with God and safe people. Invest time in relationship for yourself.

4. *Two parents help the child enter the world of other people.* A child attaches to mother first, and together they are one as far as the child is concerned. Father is supportive, but secondary. Then, late in the second year of life, father enters the picture in a more central way than before and helps the child move out of his honeymoon with mom. The child becomes interested in other relationships and begins to separate from his mother over time.

Especially in the young years, find stable, healthy opposite-sex friends, whom you aren't dating, to help your child enter the world of other people (we will deal with dating shortly). This is a very important task, as single parents often feel protective of their children and have a hard time letting their children invest in others. Church singles groups, Bible studies, and home support groups can be good sources of safe friendships, as well as being involved with loving, stable married friends.

5. *Two parents help the child move out of self-centeredness.* Over time, a child begins to see that Mom loves someone besides him. This is a new reality, and he must learn to grieve and adapt to it, sharing love and giving people freedom.

Make your home a place where, as much as possible, your child has other adults with whom to eat, play, work, and relax. Let him see you connect with others.

6. Parents also provide a check and balance on each other. When one errs, the other can correct him, and the child isn't victim to a blind spot of one parent.

Open your life to people of good character, and ask for their help with your parenting faults. Become involved in a good support group for single parents and deal with these issues.

A Word About Dating

Many single parents hope to marry or remarry one day. Marriage is a great institution, and dating is how people find a spouse. However, single parents need to deal with dating differently than they did before they had kids. Basically, you need to remember the function of dating and keep dating separate from parenting.

Dating is ultimately two people exploring whether they want to marry. It involves time, experiences together, communication of likes and dislikes, and other, similar things. Dating isn't a context in which to get your emotional needs met, nor should it be. Both parties need to preserve the freedom of the other until they both see that they want to make a deeper commitment to each other.

Some single parents will get their dates involved with their kids at the same time they are getting involved with the date. They want everyone to like everyone else. Sometimes their need for family overcomes their judgment. And sometimes they use their dating life as a source of emotional support, instead of nonromantic relationships. We believe that dating, especially in the early stages, is not a good primary place for getting deep emotional needs met. Dating is by definition unstable and experimental, as two people are testing the waters before they make a commitment to each other. Platonic relationships are more stable and reliable as your main sources of love and comfort. So we would exercise caution about letting your date get too involved with your children.

There is also a danger that your child can slip into a dependent relationship with your date. To involve your child with your date, and then for the relationship to end, can be very destructive to her needs for basic trust, stability, protection from abandonment, and a sense of responsibility for events in her life.

Enjoy your dating life. Don't hide it from your child. But you will need to think cautiously about how involved your child should be with your date, as many experts recommend keeping your kids out of the relationship unless you are headed for the altar. When you move into a deeper commitment, allow more involvement, but your date should not be taking over any parent functions unless you marry. Keep parenting and dating divided into two distinct processes.

When to Get Help

How do you know when you have encountered a parenting problem beyond your resources? So many problems—such as aggression and attitude problems—have a range of severity. God has equipped parents to solve most problems. However, sometimes you need to contact a child therapist or specialist. Here are some guidelines to follow:

Pray. Before anything else, ask your Father in heaven to help you help your child: "For the LORD gives wisdom, and from his mouth come knowledge and understanding" (Proverbs 2:6). Let him know you are struggling and are dependent on him for his help.

Stay or get connected to your child. Talking with your child can open up information you need so you can decide whether to seek professional help. Or it can help solve the problem altogether. A child's isolation and withdrawal from family are always a first warning sign of a problem. For example, if your teen is shutting herself up in her room whenever she is in the house, don't wait for her to come out of her isolation. Take initiative with her, telling her you are concerned and want to know if she is struggling. If she persists in cutting off relationship, you may want to tell her that you consider this a red light and that, if she can't talk to you, you will take her to a pastor or counselor for help.

Always make sure your child is in ongoing medical care. Sometimes behavior problems are physiological. For example, a connection has been established between strep throat and obsessive-compulsive behavior in children.

Stay in a healthy, child-wise community. Being around healthy churches with good children's and youth ministries is extremely valuable. Youth leaders and teachers who work with kids a great deal know what the normal ranges of behavior are and can help you ascertain how serious a problem really is. For example, a change in clothing style may indicate that your child is becoming a normal adolescent. But an antisocial style change may be a warning sign of a problem. For example, clothing that is sexually revealing or T-shirts with anti-life messages are something to be concerned about.

Deal with your desire to not be at fault. Your own fear of what your child or other people may think can hinder your attempt to find out your child's problem. Such fear can result in your minimizing your child's condition or blaming it on him, labeling him the "black sheep" of the family. Remember that all parents fall short in some way and that God heals the sick, not the well (Matthew 9:12–13). Give up your wish to be the perfect parent and honestly investigate whether your parenting style is part of your child's problem. For example, say to your child, "I want to work with you on finding out if I have contributed to your poor grades, and how I can change to help you change. Can you think of any way I make it hard for you to study?" Also, ask friends how you might be not structuring your child's study time, or how you might be enabling your child's bad grades. You are then truly parenting.

Investigate the problem as a character issue. Explore if your child's struggle has to do with problems with relationship, responsibility, reality, competence, talents, spiritual issues, or letting go. A problem may often be a symptom that something in a child's character growth is insufficient or breaking down. See if dealing with the character issue helps the problem. For example, if a child is struggling with a chronically rebellious attitude, explore this with him. Talk to him, his teachers, and youth pastor. His surliness may not be simply a disobedience problem. He may be struggling in some relationship. Or he may need more structure, or less. Try to identify the character issue with which he is dealing. Help him with it. See if that resolves the problem.

Give "character work" time to take effect. If you are dealing with a character issue, allow the process some time. Your child may be taking some time to figure out a reality you are helping her adapt to. For example, your toddler may not be used to Mommy putting her in time out for getting out of bed in the middle of the night. This reality is a new one for her. As far as she is concerned, you are changing the rules, and she is right. Give her time to get used to these new rules and consequences, but keep up the consequences. This is especially true with boundary issues, in which a child generally escalates her undesirable behavior for a period of time as she tests your limits. Hang on!

Get help when all the above doesn't work over time. Even with the right kinds of ingredients of grace, truth, and time, some problems go beyond normal parenting resources. Fighting, academic failure, isolation, and low motivation levels that don't get better over time are signs that you need to get more help. Find a specialist. If your child's fever gets beyond a certain point, you rush to the emergency room. It's the same in the parenting world: problems that don't go away are a symptom that something is wrong.

Look for red flags that mean "get help." Some serious issues won't improve and may worsen until an expert intervenes. Get help quickly. Such dangerous problems might include

- Infants who cry excessively and seem to be in pain
- Toddlers who are uncontrollable even with good consequences
- Very withdrawn and unsocialized children
- Kids with bizarre behavior, such as head-banging
- Preteen and teen severe weight loss, or bingeing and purging
- Violence

- Depression
- Fire-starting
- Self-mutilation, such as cutting and burning the skin
- Serious school problems, such as truancy, grades, conduct
- Drinking or drugs
- Sexual misconduct
- Ritualistic cult involvement

Fortunately, with the right interventions, many of these issues can be resolved. Some may take much time, energy, and resource. Stay connected to your own support system if you have to deal with any of these problems. And whatever you do, stay as involved as possible with your child. Many children with serious problems grow up and out of them, and establish good, productive lives because they had parents who got help in time and assisted them in working through them.

Remember, God understands the unusual stress and strain that both you and your child are going through as a single parent. He comforts and helps those in the valleys of life who look to him. Call on him for support and answers to these parenting struggles: "The Lord is the one who sustains me" (Psalm 54:4).

Conclusion

When in Doubt, Connect

I am always a little amazed when I talk to parents who have actually read parenting books from cover to cover. Parenting itself demands such a large investment of time and energy with the day-to-day crises of living, I can hardly see how folks find time to study the issue. It's like the man who accidentally closes a window on his hand. At that moment, he's not thinking about resizing the window. All he can experience is the pain. So if you've gotten this far, our hats are off to you for going deeper than the day-to-day tasks of parenting.

Raising great kids is a goal that is both overwhelming and frightening for many parents. The responsibility of someone's life in your hands, knowing your own failings, can make anyone anxious and unsure. In addition, the amount of material we have written in this book can be daunting. You may wonder if you can do all the work on character development we have presented.

To address these concerns, we want to leave you with some final thoughts. We want you to see where you are in the parenting process and to start rearing children who will one day become grown-ups who love, work, and worship well: "We are to grow up in all aspects into him" (Ephesians 4:15 NASB).

The Divine View

You need to understand your parenting from God's point of view. Remember that God chose you to be your child's parent. God chose you to be his "hands and feet" in dispensing his grace and truth to your child. You have been called with a holy calling (2 Timothy 1:9). He is helping, guiding, and supporting you. He is not surprised by the twists and turns of the process.

The job is a large one, but not too large for you and God. As Mother Teresa said, "I know God won't give me anything I can't handle. I just wish he didn't trust me so much." He trusts you with what he has given you, and he has equipped you for the task.

Not only that, but your child is also God's child. He is taking his own responsibility in the process. He will never forsake his own (Deuteronomy 31:8). He is deeply invested in your child's safety and growth. God forbid that you would ever shirk your duties to your child. But even if you did, God would not leave your child unattended: "Though my father and mother forsake me, the LORD will receive me" (Psalm 27:10). This is a comfort for you and your child.

Parents Need Support

You also need the help and support of others. You can't parent well in a vacuum. You don't have everything your child needs, and you need to get what you don't possess from warm, honest people. There are many ways to do this. For example, many churches now have parenting classes and fellowship groups. Some towns have community support for parents. Also, friends and neighbors often organize small get-togethers to trade parenting problems and tips. The keys here are that the groups need to be safe contexts in which to be open, to be centered on healthy parenting, and to meet regularly. Just as you are teaching your child to reach out to you, you need to be reaching out for resources, assistance, and encouragement. This applies not only to your parenting, but also to yourself. You need to be in regular, vulnerable contact with people who are also helping you grow.

One of the most common problems we will hear from parents who call our "New Life Live" radio program is isolation. We will tell a parent, "You need a supportive church or some relationships to help you in your parenting." So often she will say, "I've tried all the friends, churches, support groups in my area, and they are cold, or legalistic, or in denial." Whether this is true or not, it points to an important point: You cannot assume that being a parent means you are automatically in community. Take steps to find what resources are in your area for both parenting and personal-spiritual growth help.

Our book *Safe People* describes how to look for and evaluate people and groups that are spiritually and emotionally good for you. We would recommend chapter 11, "Where Are the Safe People?" which has not only information on good people, but also a section on evaluating good churches.

Use the Structure

We hope you will use this book as a roadmap pointing you to the six areas in which your child needs to be growing. Children can cause a lot of chaos, and you need to know where the parenting process is now and where it is going. No matter what age your child, familiarize yourself with the six character traits and address them. These traits can organize and focus your parenting. Talk with your spouse and other important people about them. Find ways to implement growth. Identify the areas in which your child is struggling.

For example, evaluate whether your child needs help in responsibility. Does she not attend to your requests, have trouble following through, or actively rebel? Take action to help her take responsibility for her life and help her experience loving consequences to teach her self-control.

Normalize Failure

Every parent is a bit of a perfectionist. You want to parent the right way, and you don't want your failures to hurt your children. The sad reality is that you have failed in the past and that you will fail in the future. You can't love, provide structure for, and teach your children perfectly every time. And your failures do affect your children.

However, this isn't meant to make you feel guilty. The good news is that children are resilient, and they can recover and flourish under imperfect parents. But it is much better for the child to have parents who admit failure, ask for forgiveness, and change as they learn from their errors. Be a parent who is not afraid of failure, but sees it as a way to grow. Be less afraid of mistakes and more afraid of denying them. Remember that "there is now no condemnation for those who are in Christ Jesus" (Romans 8:1). When you are not condemned, you need not be afraid of failure.

I have a friend who told me, "I knew from an early age that my parents were crazy in a couple of areas. But it was all right because they always talked about it with me, and I knew they were working on it. We all got through it okay."

When in Doubt, Connect

When you don't know what to do, what do you do? This is a question all parents face. By its nature, parenting is unpredictable because children are unpredictable. You are dealing with little human beings who are complex, impulsive, contradictory, creative, wanting total freedom, and always in transition. You probably have more memories of being at the limits of your understanding and abilities than you can count. The parent who has it all mapped out is going to be either overcontrolling or out of touch with reality.

When you encounter these periods of uncertainty, when you don't have an answer, a game plan, or a solution, the best course of action is to get connected with your children. When in doubt, connect. It never hurts, often helps, and sometimes is the entire solution to the problem.

This is not always easy. Children can be frustrating, provocative, and hurtful. Connection may not be the first thing you think of. Instead, you may try the following:

- Controlling the child
- Dealing with the problem before establishing relationship
- Attempting to use logic to show the child your point of view
- Trying to talk the child out of his feelings

- Disengaging from the child in retaliation for his disengagement from you

Relationship, as we discussed in chapter 4, is the most important of all the character aspects in this book. It is the foundation on which you build. God designed us to connect to him and to each other. Relationship is the very stuff and meaning of life. It is the source and reason for existence, just as it is the essence of God's character. At his deepest part, God is love (1 John 4:16). In being bonded we truly live.

Your child needs to be rooted and grounded in love (Ephesians 3:17), internalizing the many experiences of your empathy and comfort over time so that he lives in a state of relationship. However, childhood is a time of developing the ability to stay connected. Sometimes your child will disengage, detach, or not be able to feel your care. Other times you will withdraw your love for various reasons. For example, you may be depleted of love yourself, and pull away. Or you may be so angry that you inadvertently become cold toward her. Either way, you should make the first move toward your child when the relationship is broken.

Connection always comes first. When you encounter an unsolvable problem, take steps to move toward your children in a way that they can experience that you are with and for them and that you want to understand their internal world. They are lost in their struggle and much less able to engage you in your world than you are able to engage them in theirs. They are the children, you are the adult.

This is how God dealt with us when we were alienated from him. He didn't tell us to get our act together and then connect. He reconciled to us first, knowing we didn't have it in us to change until we were hooked up to him: "God was reconciling the world to himself in Christ" (2 Corinthians 5:19).

Here are some examples of staying in relationship to deal with problems:

Your infant cries a lot, and the doctor says he is healthy.	Hold, carry, comfort, walk, and soothe him.
Your toddler screams when you stop her from touching the electric outlet.	Hold her if she lets you, contain her hatred, and help her start to grieve and resolve. If she doesn't let you hold her, don't force the issue. Simply soothe her verbally for a while, and let her know you are there.
Your eight-year-old is brokenhearted when a best friend turns on him.	Draw him out, empathize, let him feel his sadness, and after that, problem-solve with him.
Your sixteen-year-old withdraws into her room, and you suspect drug use.	Invite her to talk, tell her you miss your relationship with her, ask if you've alienated her somehow. Connecting comes before confrontation.
Your junior in college isn't achieving his grade-point potential.	Ask to meet and talk, check out the status of your relationship and the state of his own life and struggles. Connecting comes before dealing with the GPA.

Sometimes connection solves the problem, and sometimes it is only the first of many, many steps to solve it. But of all the approaches to your child, teach him by word and deed that being in relationship is very important.

Of course, we are not saying to only connect when there are problems. That creates a problem all its own! A child who learns that the only way to be loved is to have a problem will often fail and struggle more to be connected to his parents. Keep your love sustained and constant, rooting and grounding your child in an atmosphere of care (Ephesians 3:17). Through good times and bad, make attachment the norm of your child's existence.

We are grateful that there are parents like you who desire the best for your child. May God bless you in your task, and may he complete it through you.

Henry Cloud, Ph.D.
John Townsend, Ph.D.
Newport Beach, California
1999

Acknowledgments

We would like to thank several people who were instrumental in producing this book: Our editor, Sandy Vander Zicht; our publisher, Scott Bolinder; our agent, Sealy Yates; and his associate, Tom Thompson. We deeply appreciate their hearts and efforts to help us in so many ways.

The MOPS Story

It was a Tuesday morning, at about 9:30. They had each faced spilled cereal, tangled hair, and a few had even been forced to change their outfits due to last-minute baby throw-up on a shoulder or lap. They had driven, or pushed strollers, to the church and had dropped their little ones off in the nursery. They had made it!

And now they sat, knees almost touching, in the circle of children's chairs from the Sunday school room. Hands held cups of hot coffee and doughnuts in utter freedom because this treat did not have to be shared with a child's sticky fingers. Mouths moved in eager, uninterrupted conversation. Eyes sparkled with enthusiasm. Hearts stirred with understanding. Needs were met.

That morning, in 1973, was the first morning of MOPS, or Mothers of Preschoolers. From its humble beginnings in a church in Wheat Ridge, Colorado, with only a handful of moms, MOPS International now charters approximately 2,500 MOPS groups in churches in the United States and 11 other countries. Groups meet during the day, in the evening, even on weekends.

Some 100,000 moms are touched by a local MOPS group, and thousands more are encouraged through the media arms of MOPS: MomSense radio and newsletter, MOPS' web site, and publications such as this book. MOPS groups meet the unique needs of mothers of preschoolers in a variety of settings, including urban, suburban, rural, international, and groups specifically geared to teen moms. Mission MOPS provides funds for organizations that need financial assistance for MOPS group leadership training and chartering.

MOPS grew out of a desire to meet the needs of every mother of preschoolers. Today, when a mom enters a MOPS meeting, she is greeted by a friendly face and escorted to MOPPETS, where her children enjoy their special part of the MOPS program. In MOPPETS, children from infancy through kindergarten experience a caring environment while they learn, sing, play, and make crafts.

Once her children are settled, the MOPS mom joins a program tailor-made to meet her needs. She can grab something good to eat and not have to share it! She can finish a sentence and not have to speak in Children-ese!

The program typically begins with a brief lesson taught by an older mom who's been through the challenging early years of mothering and who can share from her experience and from the truths taught in the Bible. Then the women move into small discussion groups where there are no "wrong answers" and each mom is free to share her joys and struggles with other moms who truly understand her feelings. In these moments, long-lasting friendships are often made on the common ground of finally being understood.

From here, the women participate in a craft or other creative activity. For moms who are often frustrated by the impossibility of completing anything in their unpredictable days, this activity is deeply satisfying. It provides a sense of accomplishment and growth for many moms.

Because moms of preschoolers themselves lead MOPS, the program also offers women a chance to develop their leadership skills and other talents. It takes organization, up-front abilities, financial management, creativity, and management skills to run a MOPS program successfully.

By the time they finish the MOPS meeting and pick up their children, the moms feel refreshed and better able to mother. MOPS helps them recognize that moms have needs too! And when they take the time to meet those needs, they find they are more effective in meeting the needs of their families. This is how one mom described MOPS:

> *MOPS means I am able to share the joys, frustrations and insecurities of being a mom. Our meetings provide the opportunity to hear someone else say, 'I was up all night,'*

or 'they're driving me crazy!' or 'He doesn't understand.'
While listening to others, I may discover a fresh idea or
a new perspective that helps me tackle the job of parent-
ing, home management, or being a good wife. It's impor-
tant to feel normal and not alone. Burdens are lifted
when the woman next to me says, 'I know exactly how
you feel.' MOPS is a place for my children to interact
with peers while I savor some uninterrupted conversa-
tion. I was not a Christian when I began attending
MOPS. Over the past year I have experienced tremen-
dous spiritual growth and I know that MOPS is a con-
tributor to that growth. Now, fellowship with other
Christian women is an integral reason for me to attend.
I thank the Lord for bringing me and my children to
MOPS.

The MOPS program also enables moms to reach out and
help other moms, fulfilling not only a need to belong and be
understood but a need to help others.

To receive information such as how to join a MOPS group,
or how to receive other MOPS resources such as MomSense
newsletter, call or write:

> MOPS International,
> P.O. Box 102200,
> Denver, CO 80250-2200
> Phone 1-800-929-1287
> E-mail: Info@MOPS.org.
> Web site: www.MOPS.org.

To learn how to start a MOPS group, call 1-888-910-MOPS.
For MOPS products call The MOPS Shop at 1-888-545-4040.

For information on books, resources or
speaking engagements:

Cloud-Townsend Resources
3176 Pullman Avenue, Suite 104
Costa Mesa, CA 92626
Phone: 1-800-676-HOPE (4673)
Web: www.cloudtownsend.com

Find these other resources by Dr. Cloud & Dr. Townsend at your favorite Christian bookstore.

Boundaries

This book presents a biblical treatment of boundaries, identifies how boundaries are developed and how they become injured, shows Christian misconceptions of their function and purpose, and gives a program for developing and maintaining healthy limits.

Hardcover 0-310-58590-2
Softcover 0-310-24745-4
Abridged Audio Pages® Cassette
0-310-58598-8
Unabridged Audio Pages® Cassette
0-310-24331-9
Unabridged Audio Pages® CD
0-310-24180-4
Workbook 0-310-49481-8

Boundaries (New, Revised ZondervanGroupware™)

Designed for groups of every size, here's a new, interactive edition of the successful Boundaries cirriculum. Easy-to-use Leader's Guide minimizes preparation time, while a new 120-minute video contains a brief message from the authors to group leaders and includes discussion jump-starters as well as vignettes dramatizing topics covered in the nine sessions.

Zondervan*Groupware*™ 0-310-22362-8
Participant's Guide 0-310-22453-5
Leader's Guide 0-310-22452-7

Boundaries with Kids

This book helps parents set boundaries with their children and helps them teach the concept of boundaries to their children.

Hardcover 0-310-20035-0
Softcover 0-310-24315-7
Abridged Audio Pages® Cassette 0-310-20456-9

Changes that Heal

This book focuses on four developmental tasks—bonding to others, separating from others, integrating good and bad in our lives, and taking charge of our lives—that all of us must accomplish to heal our inner pain and enable us to function and grow emotionally and spiritually. The condensed audio version of the book is read by the author.

Softcover 0-310-60631-4
Mass market 0-310-21463-7
Abridged Audio Pages® Cassette
0-310-20567-0
Workbook 0-310-60633-0

Hiding from Love

John Townsend offers help for identifying and healing from harmful withdrawal behavior and creating healthy, fulfilling relationships.

Softcover 0-310-20107-1
Workbook 0-310-23828-5

The Mom Factor

Drs. Henry Cloud and John Townsend identify six types of moms and show how they profoundly affect our lives.

Hardcover 0-310-20036-9
Softcover 0-310-22559-0
Workbook 0-310-21533-1

Safe People

Finding safe people provides the foundation for building healthy, lasting relationships. Here's how to identify safe people in your life.

Softcover 0-310-21084-4
Workbook 0-310-49501-6

Twelve "Christian" Beliefs That Can Drive You Crazy

This workbook format helps people understand twelve common but false assumptions that cripple their faith.

Softcover 0-310-49491-5

More books especially for Mothers of Preschoolers

Loving and Letting Go
Carol Kuykendall has written a much-needed book for parents who must face giving up parenting as their children grow into independent adults.

Softcover 0-310-23550-2

What Every Mom Needs
These two MOPS authorities show how mothering preschoolers can be rewarding, not frustrating, when Mom's nine needs are met.

Softcover 0-310-21920-5

Mom to Mom
Inspiration and encouragement are offered to mothers of all ages who feel inadequate to the task of mothering.

Softcover 0-310-22557-4

A Mother's Footprints of Faith
This collection of personal stories describes one woman's journey of growing closer to Jesus.

Softcover 0-310-22562-0

Getting Out of Your Kids' Faces and Into Their Hearts
This book explains how to build the strong family relationships that will win your kids over.

Softcover 0-310-48451-0

What Every Child Needs

Written in a warm, nurturing style, this book details the nine kinds of love every child needs: security, affirmation, family, respect, play, guidance, discipline, independence, and hope.

Softcover 0-310-23271-6

A Cure for the Growly Bugs and Other Tried-and-True Tips for Moms

This book is full of tips on parenting from women in MOPS groups around the country. It gives new mothers encouragement and practical ideas to help them nurture their children and gain confidence in their parenting.

Softcover 0-310-21135-2

Children Change a Marriage

This book focuses on the changes and challenges in a marriage when a husband and wife become Mom and Dad.

Softcover 0-310-24299-1

Beyond Macaroni and Cheese

MOPS groups have gathered hundreds of recipes from their members and shared practical and entertaining information for mothers and fathers who cook, especially parents of preschoolers.

Softcover 0-310-21978-7

Meditations for Mothers

This devotional includes beautiful illustrations of birds, nests, and birdhouses, and the text uses bird-related imagery to encourage moms in their relationship with God and with their families.

Hardcover 0-310-22654-6

We want to hear from you. Please send your comments about this
book to us in care of the address below. Thank you.

GRAND RAPIDS, MICHIGAN 49530

www.zondervan.com